KOREAN FOR K-POP FANS

MASTER BASICS OF HANGUL, GRAMMAR, AND PRONUNCIATION — UNDERSTAND SONG LYRICS, GET JOKES, AND SING ALONG WITH YOUR FAVORITE IDOLS

HALLYU PRESS

Cover design by Kostis Pavlou

1st Edition 2024

For Luna

목차 - TABLE OF CONTENTS

인트로/Intro 1
케이팝 팬을 위한 한국어 (keipap paen-eul wihan hangugeo)

1. 한글 (Hangul) 4
The Korean Alphabet

2. Everyday Words 17
The Essential Vocabulary

3. K-Pop Words 40
Fandom Vocabulary

4. The Basic Sentence 48
Structure & Components

5. Verbs & Conjugation 62
Where the Action Is

6. Adjectives & Adverbs 78
The Bling

7. More Sentence Structures 86
Negations & Questions

8. Everyday Phrases 106
for everyday situations

9. K-Pop Phrases 114
The Fun 130

10. The Finishing Touches 124
Comparisons, Prepositions, and Connectors

11. The Real Fun Begins 130
Putting Your Hard-Earned Skills to Work

12. Tools & Aids 137
Building on the Foundation

아웃트로/Outro 146
(You can read this now!!)

부록 - Appendix 147
참고 문헌 - References 163

인트로/INTRO
케이팝 팬을 위한 한국어 (KEIPAP PAEN-EUL WIHAN HANGUGEO)

OVER THE PAST TWO DECADES, the Korean Wave, or Hallyu, has swept across the globe, captivating hearts with its irresistible blend of music, dramas, movies, and fashion. At the forefront of this cultural phenomenon is K-pop, a music genre synonymous with passion and creativity.

If you are one of the millions of fans who can't get enough of the infectious beats, jaw-dropping performances, and charismatic idols, then this book is for you!

As a true K-pop fan, you know that learning Korean — 한국어 (hangugeo) — is the key to unlocking a deeper appreciation for your favorite artists and their work. That's where *Korean for K-Pop Fans* comes in – your ultimate guide to mastering the language and immersing yourself in the world of K-pop like never before!

You are in luck, as music is a gateway to language learning. Why, one of our staff members' immigrant mother learned English by following the lyrics sheets while singing along to her favorite Beatles songs in her teens! This demonstrates just how powerful music can be in language acquisition.

A Few Things to Keep in Mind as You Go Through This Book:

- Whenever appropriate, Hangul words and phrases are followed by romanized pronunciation in parentheses.

- As you progress through the book, challenge yourself to gradually rely less on the romanization and focus more on reading the Hangul directly. This practice will strengthen your Korean reading skills faster.
- In general, romanization of Hangul can vary; for example, the word 한글 itself can be written as "hangul" or "hangeul," so stay flexible.
- Where helpful, romanization of syllables is separated with hyphens.
- Many example phrases are accompanied by a "literal translation" in italics that preserves the original word order to help you understand sentence construction.
- There are no exercises or recaps at the end of each chapter. We packed so much information into this book that we opted to cut out redundancy. Instead, we provide useful tools and resources in Chapters 11 and 12 for self-practice and learning.
- Three **audio guides** are included for Chapters 1, 8, and 9. Scan or click (ebook only) the QR code below.

From mastering the basics of Hangul — the Korean writing system — to tackling grammar and vocabulary, this book has you covered. Each chapter is packed with relatable themes for K-pop fans, so you will be able to apply your new language skills to understanding lyrics and interviews, as well as expressing your love and support for your idols.

Just know that every language is complicated and comes with a bunch of exception-to-the-rules and idiosyncrasies. Korean is no exception. Start with the most common and useful concepts, and learn the quirky bits later as you encounter them. Remember, adaptability is the key to learning a new language!

Whether you are a new fan just discovering the addictive world of K-pop or a die-hard supporter looking to deepen your connection with your favorite idols, *Korean for K-Pop Fans* is the perfect companion on your language learning journey. Get ready to connect with fellow fans from all corners of the globe, appreciate the beauty of the Korean language and culture, and elevate your K-pop fandom experience to the next level!

What are you waiting for? Dive into *Korean for K-Pop Fans* and let the magic of K-pop and 한국어 (hangugeo, the Korean language) unfold before you. So…

시작해봐요! (si-jak-hae-bwa-yo) - Let's begin! / *Begin-let's do!*

ONE
한글 (HANGUL)
THE KOREAN ALPHABET

AS A PASSIONATE FAN, you have likely found yourself — at least trying — singing along to catchy tunes, phonetically sounding out what you think you are hearing, unsure if you are saying anything right. But fear not! Your journey to mastering Korean begins with a crucial first step: understanding Hangul, the Korean alphabet.

Hangul is a beautifully designed writing system that sets Korean apart from other East Asian languages. Unlike Chinese characters or Japanese *kanji*, Hangul is a phonetic alphabet, meaning each symbol represents a specific sound rather than a meaning. This allows non-native speakers to approach Korean much more easily.

In this chapter, we will explore the history and structure of Hangul, breaking down consonants, vowels, and their combinations. By the end of this chapter, you will have a solid understanding of Hangul and start reading and writing like a true K-pop fan.

A BRIEF HISTORY OF HANGUL

To appreciate the ingenuity of Hangul, let's take a brief look at its history. In the 15th century, during the reign of King Sejong the Great of the Joseon Dynasty, the Korean language was primarily written using Chinese characters, known as *hanja*. However, *hanja* was difficult to learn, creating a significant literacy gap between the elite and the common people.

King Sejong recognized this issue and sought to create a new writing system that would be easy to learn and use for all Koreans. In 1443, after years of research and development, King Sejong and a group of scholars unveiled Hangul, a revolutionary alphabet that would transform Korean society.

At first, Hangul was met with resistance from the elite class, who viewed it as a threat to their power and status. However, over time, Hangul gained popularity and eventually became the primary writing system for the Korean language.

Today, Hangul is celebrated as one of the most scientific and efficient writing systems in the world, a testament to King Sejong's vision and dedication to his people.

So let's get down to it!

자음(JA-EUM) & 모음 (MO-EUM) - CONSONANTS & VOWELS

The Hangul alphabet consists of 24 letters: 14 consonants and 10 vowels. In addition to these basic letters, there are 5 "double consonants" and 11 diphthongs – or "compound vowels." Each letter is designed to represent a specific sound. And these letters are combined to form "syllable blocks."

자음 (ja-eum) - *Basic Consonants:* The consonants in Hangul mirror the shape of the mouth when producing the sounds. For example, the letter ㄱ represents the sound "g" or "k," and its shape mimics the tongue touching the soft palate, or "velum," at the back of the mouth. Other consonants, such as ㄴ (n), ㅁ (m), and ㅅ (s), follow similar principles, with their shapes reflecting the positioning of the tongue, teeth, or lips.

But much of that is not very intuitive, and frankly, not very helpful, so don't spend too much time thinking about it. Let's just focus on learning these letters and their associated sounds.

The 14 Basic Consonants:

Hangul	Name of Letter	Romanized Pronunciation	Notes
ㄱ	giyeok	g/k	similar to "k" in "kind" or "g" in "go"
ㄴ	nieun	n	like "n" in "nose"
ㄷ	digeut	d/t	similar to "t" in "top" or "d" in "dog"
ㄹ	rieul	r/l	a combination of "r" and "l" sounds, similar to "r" in "run" or "l" in "love"
ㅁ	mieum	m	like "m" in "mother"
ㅂ	bieup	b/p	similar to "p" in "pack" or "b" in "boy"
ㅅ	siot	s	like "s" in "sun"
ㅇ	ieung	ng	silent when at the beginning of a syllable, but pronounced like "ng" in "sing" when at the end
ㅈ	jieut	j	similar to "j" in "jam"
ㅊ	chieut	ch	aspirated; similar to "ch" in "church"
ㅋ	kieuk	k	aspirated; similar to "k" in "kind
ㅌ	tieut	t	aspirated; similar to "t" in "top"
ㅍ	pieup	p	aspirated; similar to "p" in "pack"
ㅎ	hieut	h	similar to "h" in "hat"

ㅇ is the silent consonant that is used when a syllable block (which we will explain later) has only a vowel sound, like "ah" or "oh." In Korean, you can't use a vowel all by itself without a consonant in front, so they use this silent consonant as a placeholder. But when it is used as a final consonant at the bottom of a syllable block, it is pronounced "ng" as in "song."

Note that some of the basic Korean consonants sound almost like in-betweens of English ones as we know them.

- ㄱ is a cross between "g" and "k"
- ㄷ is a cross between "d" and "t"

- ㄹ is a cross between "l" and "r"
- ㅂ is a cross between "b" and "p"

So when you see a "g" or "k," "b" or "p," etc. in this book – and as you see them elsewhere when these sounds are romanized, e.g., on restaurant menus – keep in mind that they are basically the same and interchangeable.

쌍자음 (ssang-ja-eum) - *Double Consonants:* Double consonants, such as ㄲ (gg/kk) and ㅆ (ss), are formed by combining two single consonants to create a more emphatic sound. They are also called "tense" consonants, suggesting the way the muscles get tense when making these sounds. These double consonants often appear in onomatopoeic words (words that imitate natural sounds) or when expressing strong emotions.

The Five Double Consonants:

Hangul	Name of Letter	Romanized Pronunciation	Notes
ㄲ	ssang-giyeok	gg/kk	Tense; stronger version of ㄱ, like "k" in "kind" but you linger on the sound a bit longer (e.g. "casa" in spanish or "coeur" in french)
ㄸ	ssang-digeut	dd/tt	Tense; stronger version of ㄷ, like "t" in "top" but you linger on the sound a bit longer (e.g. "tía" in spanish or "terre" in french)
ㅃ	ssang-bieup	bb/pp	Tense; stronger version of ㅂ, like "p" in "pack" but you linger on the sound a bit longer (e.g. "padre" in spanish or "pain" in french)
ㅆ	ssang-siot	ss	Tense; stronger version of ㅅ, like "s" in "sun" but you linger on the sound a bit longer (e.g. "cebolla" in spanish or "cerise" in french)
ㅉ	ssang-jieut	jj	Tense; stronger version of ㅈ, like "j" in "jam" but you linger on the sound a bit longer

모음 (mo-eum) - *Basic Vowels:* Hangul vowels are equally intuitive, with each symbol representing a distinct vowel sound. The vowels are designed to resemble the shape of the mouth when producing the sounds. For instance, the vowel ㅏ represents the sound "a," and its shape resembles an open mouth. Other vowels, like ㅗ (o) and ㅜ (u), follow similar patterns. Again, if it doesn't make sense to you, don't worry about it. Just memorize these letters, and you'll be good.

Korean vowels maintain their distinct sounds regardless of their position in a word. Whether a vowel appears at the beginning, middle, or end of a word, its pronunciation remains consistent, unlike in English. Hangul vowels don't have special names for them, but are simply called by the sounds that they represent.

The Ten Basic Vowels:

Hangul	Romanized Pronunciation	Notes
ㅏ	ah	like "a" in "father"
ㅓ	eo	similar to "u" in "cup"
ㅗ	o	like "o" in "go"
ㅜ	u	like "oo" in "boot"
ㅡ	eu	pronounced somewhat like the 'oo' in "book" but with less rounding of the lips
ㅣ	i	pronounced like the 'ee' in "see"
ㅑ	yah	pronounced like 'ya' in "yap"
ㅕ	yeo	pronounced like 'yo' in "yonder"
ㅛ	yo	pronounced like 'yo' in "yoga"
ㅠ	yu	pronounced like 'yu' in "yule"

복합 모음 (bok-hap mo-eum) - *Diphthongs (Compound Vowels)*:
Much like double consonants, diphthongs represent certain sounds that don't exist in English. Diphthongs are combinations of two vowel sounds that glide together to create a new sound. Examples of diphthongs in Hangul include ㅐ (ae) and ㅘ (wa). Learning to pronounce these diphthongs will add depth and nuance to your Korean language skills.

The 11 Diphthongs:

Hangul	Romanized Pronunciation	Notes
ㅐ	ae	pronounced like the 'e' in "set"
ㅔ	e	pronounced like the 'e' in "never"
ㅚ	oe	pronounced like 'we' in "wet"
ㅟ	wi	pronounced like 'wee' in "week"
ㅘ	wa	pronounced like "why" but shorter, without the drawn out "y" at the end
ㅙ	wae	pronounced like 'we' in "wet"
ㅝ	wo	pronounced like 'wo' in "word"
ㅞ	we	pronounced like 'we' in "wet"
ㅢ	ui	pronounced like 'ui' in "suite"
ㅒ	yae	pronounced like 'ye' in "yet"
ㅖ	ye	pronounced like 'ye' in "yet"

Some tips that may come in handy:

- Notice that vowels that have two vertical or horizontal lines – ㅑ, ㅕ, ㅛ, and ㅠ – each begins with a "y" sound.
- Vowels ㅔ and ㅐ sound basically identical. The same goes with ㅚ, ㅙ and ㅞ as well as ㅒ and ㅖ. The only way to know when to use which vowel in a word is to memorize the spelling of the word.

음절 (EUMJEOL) - SYLLABLE BLOCKS

In contrast to the linear arrangement of characters in English, Hangul groups characters into syllabic units.

Each syllable is represented by a block, known as a *syllable block*, which consists of two or more letters that combine to form a single syllable. Hangul is a phonetic writing system, meaning that the characters represent sounds rather than meanings as Chinese characters do.

Words in Korean are composed of one or more syllable blocks, with each block representing a distinct syllable. This unique grouping of characters into syllable blocks is a fundamental aspect of the Korean writing system and sets it apart from many other writing systems around the world.

There are nine types of syllable blocks:

1. Consonant + Vertical Vowel – Ex: 차

2. Consonant + Horizontal Vowel – Ex: 무

3. Consonant + Compound Vowel – Ex: 왜

4. Consonant + Vertical Vowel + Final Consonant — Ex: 점

5. Consonant + Horizontal Vowel + Final Consonant — Ex: 음

6. Consonant + Compound Vowel + Final Consonant — Ex: 원

7. Consonant + Vertical Vowel + (Final Consonant + Final Consonant) — Ex: 많

8. Consonant + Horizontal Vowel + (Final Consonant + Final Consonant) — Ex: 뷹

9. Consonant + Compound Vowel + (Final Consonant + Final Consonant) – Although it is theoretically possible to have a syllable constructed this way, in reality, it is hardly ever used, so much so that we could not even come up with an example of actual use in a word. In other words, don't worry about this one.

받침 (batchim) - *The Final Consonant:* The final consonant added at the bottom of a syllable block is known as 받침 (batchim) in Korean, which translates to "supporting base." The presence or absence of a final consonant in a syllable determines which particles and endings should be used in a sentence. (We'll go over this later.)

Consonants change their sounds when used as final consonants in syllables. All final consonants are pronounced with one of seven sounds. Here is the list:

Final Consonants

	If you see these as final consonants...	Pronounce them as...
1	ㄱ, ㅋ, ㄲ, ㄳ, ㄺ	ㄱ (k)
2	ㄴ, ㄵ, ㄶ	ㄴ (n)
3	ㄷ, ㅌ, ㅅ, ㅆ, ㅈ, ㅊ, ㅎ	ㄷ (t)
4	ㄹ, ㄼ, ㄾ, ㅀ	ㄹ (l)
5	ㅁ, ㄻ	ㅁ (m)
6	ㅂ, ㅍ, ㅄ, ㄿ	ㅂ (p)
7	ㅇ	ㅇ (ng)

To add a bit more complexity – as if you needed it, final consonants can change the pronunciation of the syllables that immediately follow, a phenomenon known as *consonant assimilation.*

For example, when the final consonant of a syllable is followed by a syllable starting with another consonant, the pronunciation *(but NOT the writing)* of the final consonant can change to make the transition "smoother."

Examples of Consonant Assimilation:

1. ㄱ (or ㄲ, ㅋ, ㄳ, ㄺ) → ㅇ Assimilation

Ex: 막내 **(mak-nae)** is pronounced 망내 **(mang-nae)**. The final consonant ㄱ **(k)** in 막 assimilates to ㅇ **(ng)** when followed by ㄴ **(n)**.

2. ㄷ (or ㅅ, ㅆ, ㅈ, ㅊ, ㅌ, ㅎ) → ㄴ Assimilation

Ex: 첫눈 **(cheot-nun)** is pronounced 천눈 **(cheon-nun)**. Here, the final consonant ㅅ **(t)** in 첫 assimilates to ㄴ **(n)** when followed by ㄴ **(n)**, making it easier to pronounce.

3. ㅂ (or ㅍ, ㄼ, ㄿ, ㅄ) → ㅁ Assimilation

Ex: 밥물 **(bap-mul)** is pronounced 밤물 **(bam-mul)**. The final consonant ㅂ **(p)** in 밥 assimilates to ㅁ **(m)** when followed by ㅁ **(m)**.

4. ㄴ → ㄹ Assimilation

Ex: 한류 **(han-ryu)** is pronounced as 할류 **(hal-lyu)**. The final consonant ㄴ **(n)** in 한 changes to ㄹ **(l)** when followed by ㄹ **(l)**.

The first three are part of the same process called "nasalization." There are a number of other sound change rules, but don't get overwhelmed. For now, it's enough that you know these rules exist so you can revisit them when you are ready. Once you build a solid foundation, you can continue to expand on it at your own pace.

Hangul in Action

Now that you've got the basic Hangul rules down, let's go back to our list of basic consonants, double-consonants, basic vowels, and diphthongs with examples so you can see them in action.

자음 (ja-eum) - Basic Consonants:

Hangul	Example	Hangul	Example
ㄱ (g/k)	가사 (ga-sa) - lyrics	ㅇ (ng)	방송 (bang-song) - broadcast
ㄴ (n)	노래 (no-rae) - song	ㅈ (j)	제작 (je-jak) - production
ㄷ (d/t)	댄스 (daen-seu) - dance	ㅊ (ch)	춤 (chum) - dance
ㄹ (r/l)	리듬 (ri-deum) - rhythm	ㅋ (k)	콘서트 (kon-seo-teu) - concert
ㅁ (m)	멤버 (mem-beo) - member	ㅌ (t)	타이틀 (ta-i-teul) - title
ㅂ (b/p)	방탄소년단 (Bang-tan So-nyeon-dan) - BTS	ㅍ (p)	팬 (paen) - fan
ㅅ (s)	쇼 (syo) - show	ㅎ (h)	활동 (hwal-dong) - activity/promotion
ㅇ (silent)	아이돌 (a-i-dol) - idol		

쌍자음 (ssang-ja-eum) - Double Consonants:

Hangul	Example
ㄲ (gg/kk)	깡 (kkang) - spirit, determination
ㄸ (dd/tt)	떼창 (tte-chang) - group singing (by fans)
ㅃ (bb/pp)	뽀뽀 (bbobbo) - kisses
ㅆ (ss)	팬싸인회 (paen-ssa-in-hoe) - fan signing event
ㅉ (jj)	짱 (jjang) - awesome, best

모음 (mo-eum) - Basic Vowels:

Hangul	Example	Hangul	Example
ㅏ (a)	안무 (an-mu) - choreography	ㅣ (i)	인기 (in-gi) - popularity
ㅓ (eo)	에너지 (e-neo-ji) - energy	ㅑ (ya)	야광봉 (ya-gwang-bong) - light stick
ㅗ (o)	보컬 (bo-keol) - vocal	ㅕ (yeo)	연습 (yeon-seup) - practice
ㅜ (u)	무대 (mu-dae) - stage	ㅛ (yo)	요소 (yoso) - element
ㅡ (eu)	음악 (eum-ak) - music	ㅠ (yu)	유닛 (yu-nit) - unit (subgroup)

복합 모음 (bokhap mo-eum) - Diphthongs (Compound Vowels):

Hangul	Example	Hangul	Example
ㅐ (ae)	앨범 (ael-beom) - album	ㅝ (wo)	원곡 (won-gok) - original song
ㅔ (e/ae)	이벤트 (i-ben-teu) - event	ㅞ (we)	웨이브 (we-i-beu) - wave (dance move)
ㅚ (oe)	회사 (hoesa) - company, e.g., JYP, HYBE	ㅢ (ui)	의상 (ui-sang) - costume, outfit
ㅟ (wi)	위치 (wi-chi) - position, location	ㅒ (yae)	얘기 (yae-gi) - talk, story
ㅘ (wa)	좌석 (jwa-seok) - seat	ㅖ (ye)	예능 (ye-neung) - entertainment show, variety/comedy/game show
ㅙ (wae)	괜찮아 (gwaen-chan-a) - "it's OK"		

Common Challenges for English Speakers

While Korean pronunciation may seem straightforward at first glance, there are some challenges that English speakers often encounter.

1. Different sounds: Korean contains sounds that may not exist in English, such as the tense ㄲ (gg/kk) or ㅃ (bb/pp). These sounds require a different placement of the tongue or heavier pressure on the lips. Practice listening to native Korean speakers and try to imitate the way they produce these unique sounds.

2. Word stress: Unlike English, which emphasizes certain syllables in a word, Korean maintains a more consistent stress pattern. In Korean, each syllable receives equal stress, creating a rhythmic and even flow of speech. As an English speaker, you may need to practice speaking

Korean words with a more even stress pattern to achieve a more authentic pronunciation.

You will see this difference in loanwords, which are imported foreign words, such as "computer." In English, the word "computer" is pronounced with emphasis on the second syllable (com-PU-ter), whereas in Korean (phonetically spelled as 컴퓨터), no single syllable is stressed.

K-POP FUN – COMMON K-POP IDOL NAMES

Now you know enough to read and write your favorite idols' names! Here are the 22 most common names among K-pop idols and their group affiliation, in no particular order.

- 유진 **(Yujin)** - IVE, Kep1er
- 수빈 **(Soobin)** - Cosmic Girls, OH MY GIRL
- 민지 **(Minji)** - NewJeans, 4Minute
- 지수 **(Jisoo)** - BLACKPINK, Lovelyz
- 채영 **(Chaeyoung)** - TWICE, fromis_9
- 지연 **(Jiyeon)** - T-ara, Weki Meki
- 하영 **(Hayoung)** - Apink, fromis_9
- 은비 **(Eunbi)** - IZ*ONE, GFRIEND
- 수연 **(Suyeon)** - Weki Meki, fromis_9
- 보라 **(Bora)** - SISTAR, Cherry Bullet
- 은지 **(Eunji)** - Apink, GFRIEND
- 지아 **(Jia)** - miss A, Weki Meki
- 현진 **(Hyunjin)** - Stray Kids, LOONA
- 재현 **(Jaehyun)** - NCT, Golden Child
- 지훈 **(Jihoon)** - TREASURE, P1Harmony
- 민호 **(Minho)** - SHINee, Stray Kids
- 지민 **(Jimin)** - BTS, AOA
- 태용 **(Taeyong)** - NCT, NCT 127
- 진영 **(Jinyoung)** - GOT7, B1A4
- 영재 **(Youngjae)** - GOT7, B.A.P
- 지훈 **(Jihoon)** - Wanna One, TREASURE
- 우영 **(Wooyoung)** - ATEEZ, 2PM

Korean family names are monosyllabic (made of one syllable) and are placed before given names. The 20 most common family names in Korea are:

1. 김 (Kim)
2. 이 (Lee/Yi)
3. 박 (Park)
4. 최 (Choi)
5. 정 (Jung/Jeong)
6. 강 (Kang)
7. 조 (Cho/Jo)
8. 윤 (Yoon)
9. 장 (Jang)
10. 임 (Lim/Im)
11. 한 (Han)
12. 오 (Oh)
13. 서 (Seo)
14. 신 (Shin)
15. 권 (Kwon)
16. 황 (Hwang)
17. 안 (Ahn)
18. 송 (Song)
19. 전 (Jeon)
20. 홍 (Hong)

Note that the Romanization of Korean names and words can sometimes vary, so you may find slight differences in spelling across different sources. (Ex: For 한글, while "Hangeul" is closer to the correct Romanization, "Hangul" is more widely recognized internationally.)

Just for fun, see if you can figure out how to write your favorite idols' names. Then use Google to check if you got them right!

In the next chapter, we will pull together the letters we learned in this chapter to learn some essential words in Korean.

Download your pdf and audio files for Chapter 1 - Consonants and Vowels, using the QR code in the Intro.

TWO
EVERYDAY WORDS
THE ESSENTIAL VOCABULARY

WE KNOW you are eager to dive right into K-pop-specific vocabulary, but you must start with a certain level of familiarity with everyday Korean vocabulary used in common situations. Whether you're greeting someone, counting, or expressing basic emotions, you simply cannot function without knowing these fundamental words and phrases.

As a K-pop fan, you may find yourself in situations where you need to interact with native Korean speakers—at concerts, fan meetings, or even while traveling in South Korea. Having a solid grasp of everyday vocabulary will not only make your experiences more enjoyable but also demonstrate your respect for the language and culture.

Here, we'll explore everyday Korean vocabulary, including pronouns, words for people, places, and foods, as well as numbers and time expressions.

대명사 (DAE-MYEONG-SA) - PRONOUNS

Personal Pronouns: In the Korean language, pronouns are not as frequently used as in English, and they are often omitted in casual conversations when the context is clear. However, here are some common Korean subject pronouns along with their Hangul and Romanization:

Subject Pronouns

		Informal/Casual	Formal/Humble
First Person Singular	I	나 (na)	저 (jeo)
First Person Plural	we	우리 (uri)	저희 (jeo-hui)
Second Person Singular	you	너 (neo)	당신 (dangsin)*
Second Person Plural	you	너희 (neo-hui)	---*
Third Person Singular	he/she	그 (geu)/그녀 (geu-nyeo)**	
Third Person Plural	they	그들 (geu-deul)***	

The polite second person singular, 당신, is rarely used in conversations today; when it is, it can sometimes carry an ironic tone, where superficial politeness masks disdain or mockery. Instead, Korean speakers typically address others by their names or positions followed by the honorific suffix 님 (nim). For the polite second person plural, 여러분 (yeoreobun), meaning "everyone," is most commonly used.

**그, 그녀, and 그들 are literary words and practically never used in conversations. In most cases, the subject is implied; if clarification is necessary, Korean speakers will refer to a person by their name or say 그 분, meaning "that person" (polite).*

***그들 is essentially 그 (geu) paired with the all-purpose pluralizer 들 (deul). We will explore this concept later in this book.*

The possessive forms (e.g. my, your, his) and the object forms (e.g. me, us, him) are formed by simply adding the possessive particle, 의 (ui), and the object particle, 을/를 (eul/reul), respectively, to these subject pronouns. We will go over these more in detail in the section on particles later, but rest assured. It is actually very simple.

Demonstrative Pronouns - This, That, Here, and There: In Korean, there are two words for "that" and two words for "there," depending on how far or close the person, object, or place is in relation to the speaker and the listener. (The rules are the same whether the words are used as pronouns or adjectives.)

It is much easier to demonstrate this concept visually, so let's look at some illustrations:

이것 (igeot) - This (thing)

이것 refers to something that is either right by the speaker… or both the speaker and the listener.

그것 (geugeot) - That (thing)

그것 refers to something that is closer to the listener than the speaker, or something that they are thinking or discussing.

저것 (jeogeot) - That (thing) over there

저것 refers to something far from both the speaker and listener.

여기 (yeogi) - Here

여기 refers to the location where the speaker currently is.

거기 (geogi) - There

거기 refers to a location closer to the listener than to the speaker, or to a place they are discussing.

저기 (jeogi) - Over There

저기 refers to a location that is neither close to the speaker nor the listener.

"It" and "They"

In Korean, there are no exact equivalents to the English pronouns "it" and "they" as they are used in English. However, there are ways to express similar meanings using different grammatical structures and expressions.

"It" in Korean: Korean does not have a pronoun that corresponds directly to the English "it." Instead, Koreans use demonstrative pronouns ("this" or "that") or simply omit the subject when it is understood from the context. Here are a few ways to express "it" in Korean:

1. Demonstrative pronouns: 이것 (igeot) means "this," and 그것 (geu-geot) means "that." These pronouns can be used to refer to objects or concepts. It is important to note that the "t" sound at the end of both words are dropped in conversations. In short, you would hear 이거 and 그거 instead of 이것 and 그것.

2. Omitting the subject: In many cases, the subject can be omitted altogether if it is clear from the context. For example, to express "it is cold (to touch)," you can simply say 차가워 (chagawo), which means "(subject omitted) is cold."

"They" in Korean: Korean does not have a dedicated third-person plural pronoun like "they" in English. Instead, Koreans use different strategies to refer to a group of people or things. Here are a few ways to express "they" in Korean:

1. Using the plural particle 들 (deul): 들, attached to a noun or pronoun, indicates plurality. For example, 학생들 (haksaeng-deul) means "students," and 그분들 (geubun-deul) means "several of those individuals" (i.e., "they" or "them" when referring to people politely).

2. Using the word 사람들 (saram-deul): This word means "people" and can refer to a crowd or a nondescript group of individuals. For example, 사람들이 말했어요 (saram-deul-i mal-hae-sseo-yo) means "people said" or "they said."

3. Omitting the subject: Similar to expressing "it," the subject can be omitted if it is clear from the context. For example, instead of saying "they are singing," you can say 노래하고 있어요 (no-rae-ha-go i-sseo-yo), which means "(subject omitted) are singing."

In other words, there are many ways to express "it" and "they" in Korean depending on the context and the speaker's intention. The subject can often be omitted as Korean speakers rely on other grammatical structures and expressions to convey the intended meaning. (In other words, Korean is a "high context" language.)

Now, are you ready for some essential everyday words?

사람들 (SARAM-DEUL) - PEOPLE

Here's a list of terms related to people in the Korean language, along with their English meanings and romanization:

사람 (saram) - People:

- 남자 (**namja**) - man
- 여자 (**yeoja**) - woman
- 남자아이 (**namja-ai**) or 소년 (**sonyeon**) - boy
- 여자아이 (**yeoja-ai**) or 소녀 (**sonyeo**) - girl
- 어른 (**eoreun**) - adult
- 아이 (**ai**) - child
- 아기 (**agi**) or 애기 (**aegi**) - baby
- 친구 (**chingu**) - friend

가족 (gajok) - Family:

- 어머니 (**eomeoni**) - mother
- 엄마 (**eomma**) - mom
- 아버지 (**abeoji**) - father
- 아빠 (**appa**) - dad
- 언니 (**eonni**) - older sister, or any female even slightly older (used by females)
- 오빠 (**oppa**) - older brother, or any male even slightly older (used by females)
- 누나 (**nuna**) - older sister, or any female even slightly older (used by males)
- 형 (**hyung**) - older brother, or any male even slightly older (used by males)
- 동생 (**dongsaeng**) - younger sibling
- 여동생 (**yeodongsaeng**) - younger sister
- 남동생 (**namdongsaeng**) - younger brother
- 맏이 (**maji***) - eldest child; you'd expect it to pronounce it as "madi," but this is an exception where the final consonant ㄷ turns into ㅅ.
- 장남 (**jangnam**) - eldest son
- 장녀 (**jangnyeo**) - eldest daughter
- 막내 (**mang-nae***) - the youngest; example of consonant assimilation (ㄱ → ㅇ)
- 할머니 (**halmeoni**) - grandmother

- 할아버지 (**harabeoji**) - grandfather
- 이모 (**imo**) - maternal aunt
- 고모 (**gomo**) - paternal aunt
- 삼촌 (**samchon**) - uncle (on either side)
- 사촌 (**sachon**) - cousin
- 조카 (**joka**) - nephew/niece
- 남편 (**nampyeon**) - husband
- 아내 (**anae**) - wife
- 아들 (**adeul**) - son
- 딸 (**ttal**) - daughter
- 손자 (**sonja**) - grandson
- 손녀 (**sonnyeo**) - granddaughter

직업 (jigeop) - Profession/Occupation:

- 교수 (**gyosu**) - professor
- 선생님 (**seonsaengnim**) - teacher
- 학생 (**haksaeng**) - student
- 사장 (**sajang**) - company president
- 상사 (**sangsa**) - boss/supervisor
- 회사원 (**hoesa-won**) – company employee
- 직장 동료 (**jikjang dongnyo**) - coworker
- 부하 직원 (**buha jigwon**) - subordinate
- 리더 (**rideo**) or 지도자 (**jidoja**) – leader
- 의사 (**uisa**) – doctor
- 간호사 (**ganhosa**) - nurse
- 변호사 (**byeonhosa**) - lawyer
- 엔지니어 (**enjinieo**) - engineer

호칭 (HOCHING) - TITLES

Yes, there are terms in Korean that are similar to Mr., Ms., and Miss in English. These terms are often used in formal situations or when addressing someone respectfully. Here are some common examples:

1. 씨 (ssi) - This is a general honorific suffix similar to Mr., Ms., or Miss used *after* a person's name. It can be used for both men and women, regardless of marital status. For example:

- 김철수 **씨** (Kim Cheolsu-**ssi**) - Mr. Cheolsu Kim

- 박영희 **씨** (Park Yeonghui-**ssi**) - Ms. Yeonghui Park

You hear this one used all the time by idols when speaking formally, or sometimes when teasing one another in jest.

2. 님 (nim) - This is a more respectful honorific suffix used after a person's name or title. It is often used for people of higher status, such as teachers, professors, or customers. For example:

- 교수님 (gyosu-**nim**) - Professor

- 선생님 (seon-saeng-**nim**) - Teacher

- 고객님 (gogaeng-**nim**) - Customer; example of consonant assimilation (ㄱ → ㅇ)

3. 여사 (yeosa) - This term is used to address a married woman, similar to "Mrs." in English. It is often reserved for older women with grown kids and likely grandkids, as well. For example:

- 김영희 **여사** (Kim Yeonghui **yeosa**) - Mrs. Kim Yeonghui

4. 아주머니 (ajumeoni) - This term is used to address a middle-aged or older woman, often in a friendly or casual manner, similar to "lady" or "Ma'am." It can be used for both married and unmarried women. For example:

- 최 **아주머니** (Choi **ajumeoni**) - Mrs./Ms. Choi

5. 아저씨 (ajeossi) - This term is used to address a middle-aged or older man, often in a friendly or casual manner. For example:

- 이민수 **아저씨** (Lee Minsu **ajeossi**) - Mr. Lee Minsu

Cultural note on hierarchy

In Korean language and culture, hierarchy plays a crucial role in shaping social interactions, relationships, and communication. Age, social status, and profession are all factors that determine one's place in the hierarchy, and this is reflected in the language used to address and refer to others.

Koreans use different titles, such as 형 (hyung), 오빠 (oppa), 언니 (eonni), 누나 (nuna), 선배 (seonbae), and 후배 (hubae), to show respect and acknowledge the hierarchical relationship between the speaker and the person being addressed. These titles are used in addition to or *instead of* a person's name, depending on the context and the level of familiarity between the speakers.

If you follow K-pop or K-drama, after a while, you begin to notice that people address one another with these titles instead of their names quite often.

The first four words above are covered in the list of family members a few pages back, but the following terms have no exact equivalents in the English language:

- 선배 **(seonbae):** This term is used to refer to someone who is more senior or has more experience in a particular group or organization, primarily at school or work.
- 후배 **(hubae):** This term refers to someone who is more junior or has less experience in a particular group or organization.

The relationship between 선배 and 후배 is characterized by mutual respect; 선배 provide guidance, support, and mentorship to their 후배.

It is important to note that age is not the only factor in determining "선배-후배" relationships. For example, in a university setting, a student who entered the school earlier is considered a 선배 to those who entered later, regardless of their age.

In professional settings, 선배 and 후배 are used to refer to colleagues who have been with the company or organization for a longer or shorter period, respectively. You often hear members of K-pop groups referring to or addressing members of other groups under the same company with these terms.

For example, a member of TXT would address a member of BTS as 선배, since both groups belong to the same company, but BTS has been around much longer than TXT.

Furthermore, members of BLACK PINK would consider IVE their 후배. Even if the two groups belong to different companies, in the industry-wide context, newcomers would refer to anyone with a longer career as 선배.

In Korea, you always have to be mindful of where you are in the pecking order – as hierarchy affects not just pronouns and titles but also verb and adjective conjugation as we will see later in the book.

신체 부위 (SINCHE BUWI) - BODY PARTS

Now, let's take a look at the names of different body parts:

Hangul	Romanization	English	Hangul	Romanization	English
머리	meori	Head	손목	sonmok	Wrist
얼굴	eolgul	Face	손	son	Hand
눈	nun	Eye	손가락	son-ga-rak	Finger
눈썹	nun-sseop	Eyebrow	손톱	sontop	Fingernails
속눈썹	sok-nun-sseop	Eyelashes	가슴	gaseum	Chest/breast
코	ko	Nose	배	bae	Stomach/Belly
입	ip	Mouth	등	deung	Back
입술	ipsul	Lips	허리	heori	Waist
귀	gwi	Ear	엉덩이	eong-deong-i	Buttocks
이 (치아)	i (chia)	Tooth (Teeth)	다리	dari	Leg
혀	hyeo	Tongue	무릎	mureup	Knee
목	mok	Neck	발	bal	Foot
어깨	eokkae	Shoulder	발목	balmok	Ankle
팔	pal	Arm	발가락	balgarak	Toe
겨드랑이	gyeodeu-rang-i	Armpit	발톱	baltop	Toenails
팔꿈치	pal-kkum-chi	Elbow	피부	pibu	Skin
머리카락	meori-karak	Hair (on head)	뼈	ppyeo	Bone
털	teol	Hair (body hair or animal fur)	심장	simjang	Heart

Next up, a list of common place names in everyday Korean:

장소 (JANGSO) - PLACES

Hangul	Romanization	Translation	Hangul	Romanization	Translation
한국	han-guk	Korea	극장	geuk-jang	theater
서울	seoul	Seoul	체육관	che-yuk-kwan	gym
미국	mi-guk	America	수영장	su-yeong-jang	swimming pool
뉴욕	nyuyok	New York	공항	gonghang	airport
유럽	yureop	Europe	기차역	gi-cha-yeok	train station
일본	ilbon	Japan	버스 정류장	beoseu jeongnyujang	bus stop
도쿄	dokyo	Tokyo	지하철역	ji-ha-cheol-yeok	subway station
중국	jung-guk	China	주유소	ju-yu-so	gas station
홍콩	hongkong	Hong Kong	주차장	ju-cha-jang	parking lot
국가	gukga	country	도시	do-si	city
해외	hae-oe	overseas	시내	sinae	downtown
국내	gungnae	domestic	번화가	beon-hwa-ga	downtown
집	jip	home	교외	gyo-oe	suburbs
학교	hakgyo	school	시골	sigol	countryside
회사	hoesa	company/office	산	san	mountain
사무실	sa-mu-sil	office	바다	bada	sea/ocean
가게	ga-ge	store/shop	강	gang	river
슈퍼마켓	syu-peo-ma-ket	supermarket	호수	hosu	lake
백화점	baek-hwa-jeom	department store	섬	seom	island
시장	sijang	market	해변	haebyeon	beach
맛집	matjip	restaurant	교회	gyohoe	church
카페	ka-pe	café	절	jeol	temple
병원	byeong-won	hospital	연습실	yeon-seub-sil	dance studio
약국	yak-guk	pharmacy	녹음실	nok-eum-sil	recording studio
은행	eunhaeng	bank	무대	mudae	stage
우체국	u-che-guk	post office	콘서트홀	kon-seo-teau hol	concert hall
도서관	do-seo-gwan	library	경기장	gyeong-gi-jang	stadium
박물관	bak-mul-gwan	museum	돔	dom	dome
공원	gong-won	park	야외 무대	ya-oe mudae	outdoor stage
동물원	dong-mul-won	zoo	아레나	a-re-na	arena
영화관	yeong-hwa-gwan	movie theater	강당	gangdang	auditorium

음식점 [EUMSIKJEOM] - EATERIES

In case you haven't noticed, food is a rather serious business among Koreans – at least among our K-pop idols. Whenever they are together off stage, the conversation often seems to lead to discussions about the types of noodles and soups they are craving at the moment.

Korea has a diverse range of restaurants and eateries, each offering a unique dining experience. Here are some common types you can find in Korea:

- 한정식집 (**han-jeong-sik-jip**) serves traditional (and often more elaborate) Korean dishes like bulgogi, doenjang-jjigae (soybean paste stew), and dozens of banchan (side dishes).
- 고깃집 (**go-git-jip**) specializes in grilled meats, such as samgyeopsal (pork belly) and galbi (beef ribs), which diners cook themselves at the table.
- 백반집 (**baek-ban-jip**) serves set meals that typically include rice, soup, and several banchan (side dishes).
- 분식집 (**bun-sik-jip**) is a casual eatery offering quick, affordable snacks and light meals like tteokbokki (spicy rice cakes), odeng (fish cakes), and kimbap (Korean rice rolls).
- 일식집 (**il-sik-jip**) serves typical Japanese dishes like sushi, tempura, and udon noodles.
- 중국집 (**jung-guk-jip**) serves Chinese-inspired dishes adapted to Korean tastes, such as jajangmyeon (black bean noodles) and tangsuyuk (sweet and sour pork).
- 국수집 (**guk-su-jip**) serves noodles.
- 전집 (**jeon-jip**) specializes in Korean savory pancakes.
- 치킨집 (**chi-kin-jip**) serves fried chicken.
- 피자집 (**pi-ja-jip**) serves pizza.
- 햄버거집 (**haem-beo-geo-jip**) serves burgers.
- 라멘집 (**ra-myeon-jip**) specializes in traditional Japanese ramen.
- 카페 (**ka-pe**) or 커피숍 (**keo-pi-shop**) offers coffee, tea, desserts, and pastries.
- 베이커리 (**bei-keo-ri**) or 빵집 (**ppang-jip**) offers various types of baked goods.
- 바 (**ba**) or 술집 (**sul-jip**) serves alcoholic drinks and light snacks, sometimes even entrées.
- 포장마차 (**po-jang-ma-cha**) is a street food stall or kiosk where you can get a snack or a meal and sometimes alcohol.

집 (Jip) & 맛집 (mat-jip)

집 (jip) literally means "house." When used to refer to a restaurant, 집 comes after the type of dish they specialize in.

For example:

- 고기집 (gogi-**jip**) - Korean barbecue restaurant
- 설렁탕집 (seolleongtang-**jip**) - Ox bone soup restaurant
- 칼국수집 (kalguksu-**jip**) - Knife-cut noodle restaurant

맛집 (mat-jip) is also commonly used to refer to restaurants, especially the good ones. The word is a combination of 맛, which means "taste, flavor," and 집. Koreans often share their favorite 맛집, specifying the type of dish or cuisine that the place is known for, e.g., 불고기 **맛집** (bulgogi **matjip**), 파스타 **맛집** (paseuta **matjip**). Finding 맛집 is a popular activity for many Koreans. This trend is evidenced by the massive amount of social media content that specializes in just that.

음식 [EUMSIK] - FOOD

Just like elsewhere in the world, Koreans generally have three meals or 식사 (siksa) a day: 아침 식사 (a-chim siksa), 점심 식사 (jeom-sim siksa), and 저녁 식사 (jeo-nyeok siksa) — breakfast, lunch, dinner, respectively — and sometimes snacks or 간식 (gansik).

Here's a list of main categories of food in Korea and a sampling of their representative dishes. 요리 (yori) means "cooking" or "dish." (Check out the Appendix for a more extensive list of typical and popular dishes.)

밥 (bap) - Rice

Ex: 비빔밥 (bibimbap), 김밥 (gimbap)

죽 (juk) - Porridge

Ex: 전복죽 (jeonbok juk) - Porridge with abalone

면 (myeon) - Noodle

Ex: 칼국수 (kalguksu) - Knife-cut noodle soup

찌개 (jjigae), 국 (guk), 탕 (tang) - Stew, Soup, Stew with extra rich broth (served in a hot pot or stone bowl)

Ex: 순두부찌개 (sundubu jjigae) - Soft tofu stew, 감자탕 (gamja tang) - Spicy pork backbone stew

고기 요리 (gogi yori) - Meat Dishes

Ex: 불고기 (bulgogi) - Marinated grilled beef, 갈비 (galbi) - Grilled beef short ribs

해산물 요리 (haesanmul yori) - Seafood Dishes

Ex: 해물찜 (haemul jjim) - Steamed seafood, 생선구이 (saengseon gui) - Grilled fish

안주 (anju) - Side Dishes (consumed with alcohols, like bar snacks)

Ex: 만두 (mandu) - Dumplings, 파전 (pajeon) - Korean savory pancake

반찬 (banchan) - Side Dishes

Ex: 김치 (kimchi) - Spicy fermented cabbage, 나물 (namul) - Seasoned vegetables

장 (jang) - Fermented Sauce

Ex: 고추장 (gochujang) - Fermented red pepper paste

길거리 음식 (gilgeori eumsik) - Street Food

Ex: 핫도그 (hat-do-geu) - Korean-style corn dog, 붕어빵 (bung-eo-bbang) - fish-shaped pastry stuffed with sweet red bean paste (a winter-time staple)

디저트 (dijeoteu) - Dessert

Ex: 빙수 (bingsu) - milk-based shaved ice with various types of toppings, such as red beans, chopped fruit, and rice cake.

Clothes? Let's get you covered…

옷 (OT) - CLOTHES

Hangul (reading)	English	Hangul (reading)	English
바지 (baji)	Pants	넥타이 (nektai)	Tie
셔츠 (syeocheu)	Shirt	운동화 (undonghwa)	Sneakers
티셔츠 (tisyeocheu)	T-shirt	구두 (gudu)	Dress shoes
치마 (chima)	Skirt	슬리퍼 (seullipeo)	Slippers
원피스 (wonpiseu)	Dress	비옷 (biot)	Raincoat
재킷 (jaekit)	Jacket	수영복 (suyeongbok)	Swimsuit
코트 (koteu)	Coat	잠옷 (jamot)	Pajamas
스웨터 (seuweteo)	Sweater	속옷 (sogot)	Underwear
모자 (moja)	Hat	벨트 (belteu)	Belt
신발 (sinbal)	Shoes	장갑 (janggap)	Gloves
양말 (yangmal)	Socks	스카프 (seukapeu)	Scarf
청바지 (cheongbaji)	Jeans	귀걸이 (gwigeori)	Earrings
반바지 (banbaji)	Shorts	팔찌 (paljji)	Bracelet
블라우스 (beullauseu)	Blouse	목걸이 (mokgeori)	Necklace
정장 (jeongjang)	Suit	반지 (banji)	Ring (on finger)

날씨 (NALSSI) - WEATHER

Here is a list of all the weather-related words:

Hangul	Translation	Hangul	Translation
날씨 (nalssi)	weather	결빙 (gyeolbing)	freezing
일기 예보 (ilgi yebo)	weather forecast	혹한 (hokhan)	severe cold
맑음 (malgeum)	clear/sunny	춥다 (chupda)	to be cold
흐림 (heurim)	cloudy	쌀쌀하다 (ssalssalhada)	to be somewhat cold
비 (bi)	rain	따뜻하다 (ttatteuthada)	to be warm
눈 (nun)	snow	덥다 (deopda)	to be hot
우박 (ubak)	hail	폭염 (pogyeom)	severe heat
바람 (baram)	wind	습도 (seupdo)	humidity
태풍 (taepung)	typhoon	기온 (gion)	temperature
번개 (beongae)	lightning	영하 (yeongha)	below zero (Celsius)
천둥 (cheondung)	thunder	영상 (yeongsang)	above zero (Celsius)
폭풍 (pokpung)	storm	계절 (gyejeol)	season
소나기 (sonagi)	shower	봄 (bom)	spring
장마 (jangma)	rainy season	여름 (yeoreum)	summer
가뭄 (gamun)	drought	가을 (gaeul)	autumn/fall
서리 (seori)	frost	겨울 (gyeoul)	winter

숫자 (SUTJA) - NUMBERS

In Korean, two numerical systems are used concurrently: native Korean numbers and Sino-Korean numbers. Native Korean numbers are used for relatively small numbers; they are used for counting up to 99 (often much less), age, and hours. Sino-Korean numbers, derived from Chinese, are used for dates, money, a random sequence (e.g. pass-codes, phone numbers, addresses) and math, which often involves large, abstract numbers.

Understanding when to use each system is crucial to avoid confusion. This section will guide you through the basics of both systems, helping you master their applications in everyday situations.

고유어 수 (goyueo su) - Native Korean Numbers

Native Korean numbers exist for numbers 1 through 99. They are:

1	하나	hana	10	열	yeol
2	둘	dul	20	스물	seumul
3	셋	set	30	서른	seoreun
4	넷	net	40	마흔	maheun
5	다섯	daseot	50	쉰	swin
6	여섯	yeoseot	60	예순	yesun
7	일곱	ilgop	70	일흔	ilheun
8	여덟	yeodeol	80	여든	yeodeun
9	아홉	ahop	90	아흔	aheun

Traditionally, zero does not exist in native Korean numbers, as it was considered not possible to count something that did not exist.

To form two-digit numbers, just string together numbers as follows:

- 11 = 열 (yeol) + 하나 (hana) → 열하나 (yeol-hana)
- 45 = 마흔 (maheun) + 다섯 (daseot) → 마흔다섯 (maheun-daseot)
- 99 = 아흔 (aheun) + 아홉 (ahop) → 아흔아홉 (aheun-ahop)

Native Korean numbers are used in the following situations:

1. Counting small quantities (up to 99)
2. Age
3. Hours (minutes and seconds are in Sino-Korean)

Here are a few examples to illustrate the usage:

- Age: 원영은 **열아홉** 살이에요. (Wonyoung-eun **yeolahop** sal-ieyo.) - Wonyoung is 19 years old.
- Hour: **여섯** 시예요. (**Yeoseot** siyeyo.) - It's 6 o'clock.

한자어 수 (hanjaeo su) - Sino-Korean Numbers

Here are the Sino-Koeran numbers:

0	영	yeong	10	십	sip
1	일	il	20	이십	isip
2	이	i	30	삼십	samsip
3	삼	sam	40	사십	sasip
4	사	sa	50	오십	osip
5	오	o	60	육십	yuksip
6	육	yuk	70	칠십	chilsip
7	칠	chil	80	팔십	palsip
8	팔	pal	90	구십	gusip
9	구	gu	100	백	baek

It's very easy to form Sino-Korean numbers from 11 through 99. Once you memorize numbers 1 through 10, you simply combine them – just as you do in English:

- 11 = 십 (sip) + 일 (il) → 십일 (sip-il)
- 45 = 사십 (sasip) + 오 (o) → 사십오 (sasip-o)
- 99 = 구십 (gusip) + 구 (gu) → 구십구 (gusip-gu)

For large numbers, use the following:

1,000	천	cheon	a thousand
10,000	만	man	a ten-thousand (note that it is a proper noun)
100,000	십만	sipman	a ten ten-thousands
1,000,000	백만	baekman	a hundred ten-thousands
10,000,000	천만	cheonman	a thousand ten-thousands
100,000,000	억	eok	a 100 million (also a proper noun)

Sino-Korean numbers are used in the following situations:

1. Counting large quantities (100 and above)
2. Minutes and seconds
3. Dates (i.e. year, month, day)
4. Money
5. Measurements (e.g., weight, length, area)
6. Addresses including floor numbers
7. Phone numbers, passcodes, and other numeric codes
8. Math expressions, including percentages and fractions
9. Scores and grades

Examples:

- Time: **삼십**분 후에 회의 시작해요. (**Samsip**bun hu-e hoeui sijakhaeyo.) - The meeting starts in 30 minutes.
- Date: 오늘은 사월 **십오**일이에요. (Oneureun sawol **sibo**irieyo.) - Today is April 15.
- Money: 이 가방은 **이십만** 원이에요. (I gabangeun **isimman** wonieyo.) - This bag costs 200,000 won.

날짜 (NALJJA) & 시간 (SIGAN) - DATES & TIME

Dates:

In Korean, dates are expressed using Sino-Korean numbers. The correct order is year, month, and then day. Here is the formula: YYYY 년 MM월 DD일 (YYYY-nyeon MM-wol DD-il)

- YYYY: Year in Sino-Korean numbers
- 년 (nyeon): Year

- MM: Month in Sino-Korean numbers
- 월 (wol): Month
- DD: Day in Sino-Korean numbers
- 일 (il): Day
- 요일 (yo-il): Day of the week

The months in Korean are quite straightforward. All you need to do is add 월 (wol), meaning month, to numbers 1-12:

일월	il-wol	January (Month 1)
이월	i-wol	February (Month 2)
삼월	sam-wol	March (Month3)
사월	sa-wol	April (Month 4)
오월	o-wol	May (Month 5)
유월*	yu-wol	June (Month 6)
칠월	chil-wol	July (Month7)
팔월	pal-wol	August (Month 8)
구월	gu-wol	September (Month 9)
시월*	si-wol	October (Month 10)
십일월	sip-il-wol	November (Month 11)
십이월	sip-i-wol	December (Month12)

Note that for June and October, the last consonants in the numbers are dropped, so 육 (yuk) becomes 유 (yu), and 십 (sip) becomes 시 (si). This adjustment is made to avoid awkward pronunciation.

Examples:

- 2025년 4월 15일 or 이천이십오년 사월 십오일 (icheon isibo-**nyeon** sa-**wol** sibo-il) — April 15, 2025
- 1999년 12월 31일 or 천구백구십구년 십이월 삼십일일 (cheon-gubaek-gusipgu-**nyeon** sibi-**wol** samsibil-il) - December 31, 1999

South Korea uses the Gregorian calendar, so the months and days correspond to the Western calendar. However, the lunar calendar is used for major holidays like Chuseok (Korean Thanksgiving) and Seollal (Korean New Year).

While we are at it, we might as well cover the days of the week, which all end with 요일 (yo-il):

English	Hangul	Roman.	Direct Translation
Sunday	일요일	il-yo-il	Sun Day
Monday	월요일	wol-yo-il	Moon Day
Tuesday	화요일	hwa-yo-il	Fire Day
Wednesday	수요일	su-yo-il	Water Day
Thursday	목요일	mok-yo-il	Tree Day
Friday	금요일	geum-yo-il	Metal/Gold Day
Saturday	토요일	to-yo-il	Earth Day

In Korean, the day of the week comes at the end, unlike in English. For example:

- Saturday, May 16, 2009 = 2009년 5월 16일 토**요일** (i-cheon-gu-nyeon o-wol sip-yuk-il to-**yo-il**)

Time

Just when you thought you were getting the hang of it, it's time to cover time in Korean... Let's first go over the vocabulary:

- 시간 (**sigan**): time or x number of hours
- 시 (**si**): o'clock; hour
- 분 (**bun**): minute
- 초 (**cho**): second
- 오전 (**ojeon**): A.M. (comes before the hour and minute)
- 오후 (**ohu**): P.M. (comes before the hour and minute)
- 정오 (**jeong-o**): noon
- 자정 (**jajeong**): midnight

The effort you have put into learning two systems of numbers now comes in handy, as you need both to express time – native Korean for the hours and Sino-Korean for minutes and seconds.

Here are the hours using native Korean numbers:

1 o'clock	한 시	han si
2 o'clock	두 시	du si
3 o'clock	세 시	se si
4 o'clock	네 시	ne si
5 o'clock	다섯 시	daseot si
6 o'clock	여섯 시	yeoseot si
7 o'clock	일곱 시	ilgop si
8 o'clock	여덟 시	yeodeol si
9 o'clock	아홉 시	ahop si
10 o'clock	열 시	yeol si
11 o'clock	열한 시	yeol-han si
12 o'clock	열두 시	yeol-du si

(Note that the final sound of the numbers one through four are dropped.)

The correct order of words is AM/PM, hour, minute, and seconds (if you need to be so specific). For example:

- 오후 다섯 시 이십사 분 (ohu daseot si isipsa bun) — 5:24 P.M.

단위 명사 (DANWI MYEONGSA) - COUNTERS

In Korean, the concept of counters is crucial for counting objects, people, animals, and various other things. In English, you can simply say "three books" or "five people," but in Korean, you have to use a specific counter word for each type of object. This is somewhat like saying "a pair of shoes" or "a glass of water" in English–only far more elaborate.

Counting with Counters: The general structure for counting with counters is as follows: **Noun** (singular) + **Number** + **Counter**

For example:

- 아이돌 두 **명** (aidol du **myeong**) - two idols
- 마이크 세 **개** (maikeu se **gae**) - three microphones
- 고양이 한 **마리** (goyangi han **mari**) - one cat

Common Counters in Korean

Counter		Used for:	Example
개	gae	things	야광봉 한 개 (yagwangbong han gae) - one light stick
명	myeong	people	학생 두 명 (haksaeng du myeong) - two students
사람	saram	people (much less commonly used)	저희 세 사람 (jeohui se saram) - us three
마리	mari	animals	고양이 한 마리 (goyangi han mari) - one cat
권	gwon	books, magazines, or volumes	책 네 권 (chaek ne gwon) - four books
장	jang	flat sheet-like objects (e.g. photos, tickets, towels)	종이 다섯 장 (jongi daseot jang) - five sheets of paper
대	dae	vehicles and machinery	자동차 두 대 (jadongcha du dae) - two cars
병	byeong	bottles	물 세 병 (mul se byeong) - three bottles of water
잔	jan	cups, glasses, or mugs	커피 한 잔 (keopi han jan) - one cup of coffee
벌	beol	clothes	옷 두 벌 (ot du beol) - two pieces of clothing
송이	songi	flowers or bunches of fruit	꽃 세 송이 (kkot se songi) - three flowers
가지	gaji	types or kinds	세 가지 (se gaji) - three kinds/types
번	beon	occurrences or ordinal numbers	두 번 (du beon) - Twice; 십 번 (sip beon) - Number 10
절	jeol	verses in a song	일절 (Iljeol), 이절 (Ijeol)... - Verse 1, Verse 2...
그루	geuru	trees and plants	나무 다섯 그루 (namu daseot geuru) - Five trees
켤레	kyeolle	pairs (shoes, gloves, socks)	양말 한 켤레 (yangmal han kyeolle) - One pair of socks
벌	beol	sets of clothes and suits	정장 한 벌 (jeongjang han beol) - One suit
조각	jogak	pieces/slices of things, usually food	피자 세 조각 (pija sae jogak) - Three slices of pizza
층	cheung	floors in a building	3층 (sam cheung) - Third floor

Understanding counters might initially seem foreign. With practice, however, it will become second nature. You will be able to appreciate the nuances of the Korean language all the better.

Now that we have covered the essential everyday vocabulary, we are ready to dive into the exciting world of K-Pop in earnest. In the next chapter, we will explore specific words and concepts that will bring you closer to the vibrant K-Pop culture you love.

THREE
K-POP WORDS
FANDOM VOCABULARY

K-POP IS NOT JUST a musical genre; it is a vibrant culture with its own unique language. To truly enjoy your favorite songs and performances, you want to understand the jargon used by the industry and the fan community.

In this chapter, we will explore the fascinating world of K-pop-specific vocabulary. You will learn the terms for song structure, choreography, and other important aspects of K-pop performance. We will delve into the rich lexicon of fandom culture, so you can engage confidently with fellow enthusiasts.

케이팝 업계 관계자 (KE-I-PAP EOP-GYE GWAN-GYE-JA) - K-POP INDUSTRY PLAYERS

- 기획사 (gi-hoek-sa) - **Entertainment Company**: A business entity responsible for training, managing, and promoting K-pop artists. They provide resources for music production, marketing, and public relations, playing a pivotal role in an idol's career development. Ex: SM Entertainment, YG Entertainment, and JYP Entertainment.
- 아이돌 (a-i-dol) - **Idol**: A K-pop artist who has debuted. (Every idol considers him/herself to be an employee of their company.)

- 솔로 아티스트 **(sol-lo a-ti-seu-teu) - Solo Artist**: An individual performer who performs independently, without being part of a group.
- 연습생 **(yeon-seup-saeng) - Trainee**: An aspiring artist who undergoes rigorous training in singing, dancing, and other performance skills under an entertainment company's program, preparing for potential debut as an idol.
- 선배 **(seon-bae) - Senior**: Senior or mentor in the industry.
- 후배 **(hu-bae) - Junior**: Junior or mentee in the industry.
- 프로듀서 **(peu-ro-dyu-seo) - Producer**: A person who oversees the music production.
- 작곡가 **(jak-gok-ga) - Composer**
- 안무가 **(an-mu-ga) - Choreographer**
- 연예인 **(yeon-ye-in) - Entertainer**
- 공연자 **(gong-yeon-ja) - Performer**
- 음악가 **(eum-ag-ga) - Musician**
- 스타 **(seu-ta) - Star**
- 에이스 **(e-i-seu) - Ace**: An idol who excels in multiple areas and is a standout performer.
- 올라운더 **(ol-la-un-deo) - All-Rounder**: An idol proficient in multiple skills, such as singing, dancing, and rapping.
- 글로벌 앰배서더 **(geul-lo-beol aem-bae-seo-deo) - Global Ambassador**: An idol who represents and promotes an international fashion brand.

멤버와 역할 (MEM-BEO-WA YEOK-HAL) - MEMBERS AND ROLES

- 메인 보컬 **(me-in bo-keol) - Main Vocalist**: The most skilled and prominent singer in the group.
- 리드 보컬 **(ri-deu bo-keol) - Lead Vocalist**: Among the best singers of the group, but rank below the main singer.
- 메인 댄서 **(me-in daen-seo) - Main Dancer**: The most skilled and prominent dancer in the group.
- 리드 댄서 **(ri-due daen-seo) - Lead Dancer**: Among the best dancers of the group, but rank below the main dancer.
- 메인 래퍼 **(me-in rae-peo) - Main Rapper**: The most skilled and prominent rapper in the group.
- 리드 래퍼 **(ri-deu rae-peo) - Lead Rapper**: Among the best rappers of the group, but rank below the main rapper.
- 비주얼 **(bi-ju-eol) - Visual**: The most physically attractive member in the group.

- 막내 (mak-nae → mang-nae) - "Maknae"/The Youngest: The youngest member in the group.
- 그룹 리더 (geu-rup ri-deo) - Group Leader: The member responsible for guiding and representing the group.
- 오빠 (o-ppa) - "Oppa"/Older Brother: A term used by female artists and fans to refer to older male idols.
- 언니 (eon-ni) - "Unnie"/Older Sister: A term used by female artists and fans to refer to older female idols.
- 형 (hyeong) - "Hyung"/Older Brother: A term used by male artists and fans to refer to older male idols.
- 누나 (nu-na) - "Noona"/Older Sister: A term used by male artists and fans to refer to older female idols.
- 형 라인 (hyeong ra-in) - Hyung Line/the Older Line: The older members of a K-pop group, often taking on a mentor or leader role for the younger members.
- 막내 라인 (mang-nae ra-in) - Maknae Line/the Younger Line: The younger members of a K-pop group, typically characterized by their youthful energy and charm.
- 서브 유닛 (seo-beu yu-nit) - Sub-Unit: Smaller group formed within a K-pop group. Ex: Each of SEVENTEEN's 13 members is assigned to one of their three sub-units – vocal, performance, and hip-hop.
- 오티 (o-ti) - OT: Stands for "One True"; indicates support for the original lineup of a group. Ex: OT8 refers to all eight members of a group, emphasizing support for the entire lineup.

팬덤 용어 (PAENDEOM YONG-EO) - FANDOM TERMS

- 팬 (paen) - Fan: A person who supports and follows a K-pop artist or group.
- 스탠 (seu-taen) - Stan: A particularly dedicated and enthusiastic supporter of an artist or group; combination of "stalker" and "fan."
- 사생팬 (sa-saeng-paen) - "Sasaeng": An overly obsessive fan who invades the privacy of K-pop idols.
- 안티 팬 (an-ti paen) - Anti-Fan: Someone who strongly dislikes or criticizes a particular K-pop artist or group.
- 바이어스 (ba-i-eo-seu) - Bias: Your favorite member in a K-pop group.

- 바이어스 레커 **(ba-i-eo-seu re-keo) - Bias Wrecker**: A member of a K-pop group who unexpectedly catches your attention and makes you question your loyalty to your original bias.
- 팬덤 이름 **(paen-deom i-reum) - Fandom Name**: The unique nickname given to the fans of a particular K-pop group or artist. Ex: ARMY(s) for BTS; BLINK(s) for BLACKPINK.
- 응원 **(eungwon) - cheer, support, or encouragement**: Fanchants and cheering during performances.
- 팬챈트 **(paen-chaen-teu) - Fanchant**: A chant sung by fans during live performances, typically featuring the members' names.
- 팬카페 **(paen-ka-pe) - Fan Cafe**: Official online community for fans of a K-pop group.

음악 용어 (EUMAK YONG-EO) - MUSIC TERMS

- 음악 **(eumak) - Music**
- 노래 **(norae) - Song**
- 사랑 노래 **(sarang norae) - Love song**
- 데뷔 **(dae-bwi) - Debut**: The first official release or performance by a new K-pop artist or group.
- 컴백 **(keom-baek) - Comeback**: The release of a new song or a new album by a K-pop artist or group.
- 올킬 **(ol-kil) - All-kill**: A song that reaches #1 on all major Korean music charts simultaneously.
- 앨범 **(ael-beom) - Album**: A collection of songs released together.
- 미니 앨범 **(mi-ni ael-beom) - Mini Album**: An album with fewer tracks than a full studio album, typically containing 4-7 songs.
- 리패키지 앨범 **(ri-pae-ki-ji ael-beom) - Repackage Album**: A re-release of an album with new packaging, often including new tracks.
- 싱글 **(sing-geul) - Single**: A song released individually rather than as part of an album.
- 믹스 테이프 **(mik-seu te-i-peu) - Mix Tape**: A compilation of songs, often released for free.
- 솔로 **(sol-lo) - Solo**: Individual release by a member of a K-pop group.
- 오리지널 사운드트랙 **(o-ri-ji-neol sa-un-deu-teu-raek) - OST**: Original Soundtrack, featuring K-pop idols.

- 콜라보 (kol-la-bo) - **Collabo**: Short for "collaboration," where artists work together on a project.
- 앵콜 (aeng-kol) - **Encore**: Extra songs performed at the end of a concert.
- 절 (jeol) - **Verse**: The part of a song that tells a story.
- 후렴 (hu-ryeom) - **Chorus**: The repetitive and catchy part of a song that usually contains the main message.
- 브리지 (beu-ri-ji) - **Bridge**: A section of a song that provides contrast to the verse and chorus.
- 리듬 (ri-deu-m) - **Rhythm**
- 가사 (ga-sa) - **Lyrics**
- 멜로디 (mel-lo-di) - **Melody**

공연 (GONG-YEON) & 콘텐츠 (KON-TEN-CHEU) - PERFORMANCE AND CONTENTS

- 콘서트 (kon-seo-teu) - **Concert**
- 시상식 (si-sang-sik) - **Award Show**
- 예능 (ye-neung) - **Variety Show**
- 음악 프로그램 (eum-ak peu-ro-geu-raem) - **Music Show**: Live performance on TV.
- 뮤직 비디오 (myu-jik bi-di-o) - **Music Video**
- 쇼케이스 (syo-ke-i-seu) - **Showcase**: Pre-release live performance for media and fans.
- 댄스 연습 영상 (daen-seu yeon-seup yeong-sang) - **Dance Practice**: Videos showing idols perform the full choreography in dance studios, wearing casual workout/athleisure outfit.
- 특별 공연 (teukbyeol gongyeon) - **Special Performance**: A unique or one-time performance often for special occasions.
- 티저 (ti-jeo) - **Teaser**: Short promotional video or image.
- 릴레이 댄스 (ril-le-i daen-seu) - **Relay Dance**: Dance challenge where members in line take turns dancing to a song for fun.
- 팬캠 (paen-kaem) - **Fan Cam:** - video recording of a performance, usually at a concert or live event, that focuses on a single performer or member of a group
- 브이 라이브 (beu-i ra-i-beu) - **V Live**: A live streaming app where K-pop idols interact with fans in real-time. (V Live has been fully integrated into the Weverse platform as of the end of 2022.)
- 비하인드 (bi-ha-in-deu) - **Behind the Scenes**: Footage

showing what happens behind the scenes during the production of music videos, concerts, etc.
- 메이킹 (me-i-king) - Making Of: A video that shows the process of creating a music video, album, etc.
- 하이터치 이벤트 (ha-i-teo-chi i-beon-teu) - Hi-Touch Event: A fan event where fans get to high-five their idols.
- 팬미팅 (paen-mi-ting) - Fan Meeting: A gathering where fans get to interact with their favorite idols.
- 월드 투어 (wol-deu tu-eo) - World Tour
- 녹음 (nog-eum) - Recording
- 촬영 (chwa-ryeong) - Filming
- 립싱크 (lip-sing-keu) - Lip Sync: Mimicking singing by moving the lips in sync with a pre-recorded song.
- 라이브 (ra-i-beu) - Live

장소 (JANG-SO): VENUES/PLACES

- 경기장 (gyeong-gi-jang) - Stadium
- 뮤직홀 (myu-jik-hol) - Music Hall
- 무대 (mu-dae) - Stage
- 백스테이지 (baek-seu-te-i-ji) - Back Stage
- 녹음실 (nogeum-sil) - Recording Studio
- 연습실 (yeon-seup-sil) - Practice Room
- 댄스 스튜디오 (daen-seu seu-tu-dio) - Dance Studio
- 기숙사 (gi-suk-sa)- Dormitory: A residence provided by entertainment companies where K-pop trainees and idols live. Dormitories are great for coordinating/managing busy schedules, and fostering a team environment. They often come equipped with amenities to support their rigorous lifestyles.

팬과 소통 (PAEN-GWA SO-TONG) - FAN ENGAGEMENT

- 팬서비스 (paen-seo-bi-seu) - Fan Service: Interactions between idols and fans designed to please the fans.
- 응원봉 (eung-weon-bong) - Light Stick: A special light-up wand used by fans during concerts to show their support for their group. Each group has its own unique design.
- 팬 굿즈 (paen gut-jeu) - Fan Merch ("Goods"): Merchandise sold to fans, such as clothing, accessories, and other items.

- 커플 **(keo-peul) - "Ship"**: The practice of imagining a romantic or special relationship between two idols.
- 애교 **(ae-gyo) - "Aegyo"**: Cutsy and charming behavior, often exhibited through facial expressions, gestures, and a higher-pitched voice.
- 스킨십 **(seu-kin-sip) - "Skinship"**: Physical contact between members of a group, often seen as fan service.
- 멘트 **(men-teu) - "Ment"**: Short for "comment," refers to the talking segments during K-pop events such as concerts where idols interact with the audience.
- 첼린지 **(chael-lin-ji) - Challenge**: A dance or performance challenge, typically initiated on social media platforms.
- 미션 **(mi-syeon) - Mission**: Specific tasks or challenges — often silly — assigned to idols during variety shows, fan meetings, or promotional events.

기타 용어 (GITA YONG-EO) - MISCELLANEOUS TERMS

- 마이크 **(ma-i-keu) - Microphone**
- 스포트라이트 **(seu-po-teu-ra-i-teu) - Spotlight**
- 무대 의상 **(mu-dae ui-sang) - Stage Costume/Outfit**
- 대상 **(dae-sang) - Grand Prize**: The highest award given at Korean music awards shows.
- 세대 **(se-dae) - Generation**: A term used to categorize K-pop groups based on their debut year and style. Ex: 4세대 (sa-se-dae) - 4th Generation; groups that debuted around 2018-2022, including Stray Kids, ATEEZ, and ITZY.
- 활동 중단 **(hwal-dong jung-dan) - Hiatus**: A break or pause in a K-pop group's or member's activities, often triggered by a controversy.
- 재능 **(jae-neung) - Talent**
- 기술 **(gi-sul) - Skill**
- 카리스마 **(ka-ri-seu-ma) - Charisma**
- 스웨그 **(seu-we-geu) - Swag**: The coolness or confidence that an idol displays.
- 한류 **(han-ryu → hal-lyu) - Hallyu**: Literally the "**Korean wave**," referring to the global popularity of South Korean pop culture.
- 손가락 하트 **(son-ga-rak ha-teu) - Finger Heart**: A popular hand gesture (as seen on the cover of this book) where the thumb and index finger are crossed to form the shape of a

heart. This gesture symbolizes love, and it is often used by idols to show their appreciation for their fans. It has become an iconic symbol of the connection between K-pop artists and their supporters.

시상식 (SISANGSIK) - AWARD SHOWS

In the K-pop industry, artists strive for Daesang, or "top prize" in Korean. These awards are presented during award shows such as:

1. 골든 디스크 어워드 (Goldeun Diseukeu Eowodeu)/Golden Disc Awards (GDAs) - Often referred to as the Korean equivalent of the Grammy Awards, this ceremony recognizes outstanding achievements in the music industry.

2. 엠넷 아시안 뮤직 어워드 (Emnet Asian Myujik Eowodeu)/Mnet Asian Music Awards (MAMAs) - An annual event that honors the best in music, primarily K-pop, with categories like Artist of the Year and Song of the Year.

3. 멜론 뮤직 어워드 (Mellon Myujik Eowodeu)/Melon Music Awards (MMAs) - Another major awards show focusing on digital sales and fan votes to determine the winners.

4. 서울가요대상 (Seoul Gayo Daesang)/Seoul Music Awards (SMAs) - Celebrates the best music releases and artists of the year.

5. 한국 대중 음악상 (Hanguk Daejung Eumaksang)/Korean Music Awards (KMAs) - Focuses on artistic achievement rather than commercial success, recognizing a wide range of musical genres.

6. 아시아 아티스트 어워즈 (Asia Atiseuteu Eowodeu)/Asia Artist Awards (AAA) - Another prestigious event notable for awarding both Korean and international artists, reflecting the broad appeal of K-pop and Korean entertainment globally.

So there you have it—the essential terminology every true K-pop fan should know. Now, let's take the next step in your journey: forming sentences!

FOUR
THE BASIC SENTENCE
STRUCTURE & COMPONENTS

UNDERSTANDING sentence structure is fundamental to communicating effectively in any language. As a K-pop fan, you may have suspected that Korean sentences are structured differently from English ones, and that is indeed the case. Korean follows a word order that is different from any European language and uses "particles" to indicate grammatical relationships between words.

In this chapter, we will explore the basic components of Korean sentences, including word order, particles, and formal versus informal speech styles. Once you master these concepts, you will be able to engage in conversations in no time.

Whether you are writing a fan letter to your bias or practicing Korean with fellow fans, understanding sentence structure will help you express yourself clearly and accurately.

SUBJECT-OBJECT-VERB (SOV) WORD ORDER

One of the most important things to understand about Korean sentence structure is that it follows a Subject-Object-Verb (SOV) word order. This means that the subject of the sentence comes first, followed by the object, and finally, the verb. In contrast, English sentences typically follow a Subject-Verb-Object (SVO) word order.

Here's an example to illustrate the difference:

- *English:* I eat an apple — **S** (I), **V** (eat), **O** (an apple)
- *Korean:* 저는 사과를 먹어요. (jeo-neun sagwa-reul meogeoyo) — **S** (jeo, I)+particle (neun), **O** (sagwa, apple)+particle (reul), **V** (meogeoyo, eat)

In the Korean sentence, the subject 저 (jeo) comes first, followed by the object 사과 (sagwa), and finally the verb 먹어요 (meogeoyo). The extra letter, 는 (neun), attached to the subject and the extra letter, 를 (reul), attached to the object are called "particles." We will cover particles in depth in a moment.

Here are some more examples to get you familiarized with the basic Korean sentence structure:

- 아이유가 솔로 곡을 불러요 (Aiyu-ga sollo gogeul bulleoyo.): *Aiyu-solo song-sings* = IU sings a solo song.
- 뉴진스가 무대를 준비해요 (Nyujinseu-ga mudae-reul junbihaeyo.): *NewJeans-stage-prepares* = NewJeans prepares the stage.
- 피원하모니가 팬들에게 인사해요 (Piwonhamoni-ga paendeurege insahaeyo.): *P1Harmony-fans-greets* = P1Harmony greets the fans.
- 트와이스가 안무를 연습해요 (Twice-ga anmu-reul yeonseubhaeyo.): *Twice-choreography-practices* = Twice practices the choreography.
- 엑소가 공연을 해요 (EXO-ga gongyeon-eul haeyo.): *EXO-concert-performs* = EXO performs a concert.
- 세븐틴이 팬미팅을 해요 (Seventeen-i paenmiting-eul haeyo.): *SEVENTEEN-fan meeting-holds* = SEVENTEEN holds a fan meeting.
- 레드벨벳이 새 앨범을 발표해요 (Red Velvet-i sae aelbeom-eul balpyohaeyo.): *Red Velvet-new album-releases* = Red Velvet releases a new album.
- 아이즈원이 인터뷰를 해요 (Aijeuwon-i inteobyu-reul haeyo.): *I*ZONE-interview-gives* = IZ*ONE gives an interview.
- 스트레이 키즈가 상을 받아요 (Seuteurei Kijeu-ga sang-eul badayo.): *Stray Kids-award-receives* = Stray Kids receives an award.

Understanding the SOV word order is essential for constructing grammatically correct sentences in Korean. It may take some practice to get used to this word order, especially if you are more familiar with the

SVO structure of English. But with time and exposure, it will become more natural.

조사 (JOSA) - PARTICLES

Did you notice the presence of 가 **(ga)**, 이 **(i)**, 를 **(reul)**, and 을 **(eul)** in those sentences by any chance ? Those are some of the many particles, essential to constructing proper sentences in the Korean language. So let's go over them.

In Korean, as seen in some other Asian languages, particles are small words that are attached at the end of nouns, pronouns, or other words to indicate their grammatical function in a sentence. Particles play a crucial role in Korean sentence structure by clarifying the relationships between words and helping to convey the intended meaning. They have no perfect equivalents in European languages, so you need to buckle down a bit to grasp the concept.

Here are some of the most common particles:

는/은 (neun/eun): Topic Particles

Topic particles literally indicate the topic of a sentence. They help to highlight what the sentence is about, providing a sense of focus or emphasis on the topic.

는 (neun) and 은 (eun) are the same particle, except you use 는 after words ending with vowels and 은 after words ending with consonants.

Functions of 는/은 (neun/eun):

1. *Introducing a Topic:*

- 오늘은 엔하이픈 콘서트가 있어요. (Oneul-**eun** Enhaipeun konseoteuga isseoyo.) - As for today, there is a ENHYPEN concert.

The particle 은 (eun) introduces 오늘, or "today," as the topic of the sentence.

2. *Emphasizing Contrast:*

- 저는 르세라핌 좋아해요. (Jeo-**neun** Leuserapim-reul joahaeyo.) - I like LE SSERAFIM.

- 친구는 있지를 좋아해요. (Chingu-**neun** Itji-reul joahaeyo.) - My friend likes ITZY.

The particle 는 (neun) in both 저는 (jeo-neun) and 친구는 (chingu-neun) are used to contrast the speaker's preference with their friend's preference.

3. *General Statements:*

- 아이돌은 인기가 많아요. (Aidol-**eun** ingiga manayo.) - Idols are very popular.

The particle 은 (eun) in 아이돌은 (aidol-eun) suggests that the statement is a general observation about idols.

가/이 (ga/i): Subject Particles

These are particles used to mark the subject of a sentence. They help identify the subject of the sentence, introduce new information, or emphasize the subject in a neutral manner.

가 (ga) and 이 (i) are the same, except 가 follows vowels and 이 follows consonants.

Functions of 가/이 (ga/i):

1. Identifying the Subject:

- 싸이가 춤춰요. (Ssai-**ga** chumchwoyo.) - PSY is dancing.

The particle 가 (ga) in 싸이가 (ssai-ga) identifies "PSY" as the subject of the sentence.

2. Introducing New Information:

- 팬이 무대에 올라왔어요. (Paen-**i** mudae-e olla-wasseoyo.) - A fan came up on the stage.

The particle 이 (i) in 팬이 (paen-i) introduces 팬, or "a fan," as new information.

3. Emphasizing the Subject in a Neutral Manner:

- 제가 콘서트를 봐요. (Jae-**ga** konseoteureul bwoyo.) - I watch concerts.

The subject particle 가 (ga) in 제가 (jega) emphasizes that it is "I" who watches concerts.

Note on 는/은 *(neun/eun)* vs. 가/이 *(ga/i)*

The choice between 는/은 (neun/eun) and 가/이 (ga/i) depends on whether the subject is the topic of the sentence or not. If the subject of the sentence is the topic, use 는/은. If the subject is not the topic or is being introduced for the first time, use 가/이.

Confused? You are not alone. One of the most confusing aspects of Korean grammar for beginners is learning the difference between 는/은 and 가/이 and how to use them appropriately. Let's look at some examples (and note that the sentences follow the SOV structure):

- 정국은 막내입니다 (Jeongguk-**eun** maknae-imnida) – Jungkook is **a maknae** (the youngest in a group); a general statement identifying his position in the group. (Remember, there are as many maknaes as there are K-pop groups in the industry.)
- 정국이 막내입니다 (Jeongguk-**i** maknae-imnida) - **Jungkook** is the maknae; a statement identifying Jungkook, in particular, as the maknae of his group, not somebody else. (We will cover -imnida and other verb endings later.)

Here is another one:

- 연준은 TXT를 떠났습니다. (Yeonjun-**eun** TXT-reul tteonasseumnida) – Yeonjun **left TXT**; this simply states that Yeonjun left his group.
- 연준이 TXT를 떠났습니다 (Yeonjun-**i** TXT-reul tteonasseumnida) – **Yeonjun** left TXT; this identifies/singles out Yeonjun as the one who left his group, not somebody else.

The difference depends on what part of the statement should be emphasized. In English, the difference between "a" and "the" can serve a similar function.

There are a lot more complicated rules and exceptions to them than we can cover here. But for now, it is good enough that you are aware of the basic concept. Once you are aware, you will start to notice them in speech and writing as you watch videos – and the more you get exposed to them, the more intuitive it will become. Be patient and don't drive yourself crazy trying to get everything right from the start.

를/을 (reul/eul): Object Particles

These are object particles used to mark the direct object in a sentence. They help to clarify what the action of the verb is being performed on.

를 (reul) and 을 (eul) are the same, except you use 를 after vowels and 을 after consonants.

Examples:

- 노래를 (norae-**reul**) - song (as the object)
- 춤을 (chum-**eul**) - dance (as the object)

Objective pronouns are also formed by attaching the object particles to the personal pronouns introduced at the beginning of Chapter 2:

		Informal/Casual	Formal/Humble
First Person Singular	me	나를 (na-reul)	저를 (jeo-reul)
First Person Plural	us	우리를 (uri-reul)	저희를 (jeohui-reul)
Second Person Singular	you	너를 (neo-reul)	당신을 (dangsin-eul)
Second Person Plural	you	너희를 (neohui-reul)	---*
Third Person Singular	him/her	그를 (geu-reul)/그녀를 (geunyeo-reul)**	
Third Person Plural	them	그들을 (geudeul-eul)**	

The polite second person singular, 당신을, is rarely used in conversations today. Instead, Korean speakers typically address others by their names or positions followed by the honorific suffix 님 (nim). For the polite second person plural, 여러분을 (yeoreobun-eul), meaning "everyone," is most commonly used.

**그를, 그녀를, and 그들을 are literary words and practically never used in conversations. In most cases, the subject is implied; if clarification is necessary, Korean speakers will refer to a person by their name or say 그 분, meaning "that person" (polite).*

들 (deul): Plural Particle

The particle 들 indicates plurality. Although not incorrect, it is rare to see 들 used for inanimate objects like books or cups. 들 is primarily used for people and can sometimes be used for animals and plants (excluding those that have already been caught or harvested that you buy in stores).

Inanimate objects are either left unpluralized or their quantity is specified using counters.

Examples:

- 사람 (saram)/person → 사람들 (saram-**deul**)/people
- 친구 (chingu)/friend → 친구들 (chingu-**deul**)/friends

Example Sentences:

- 아이돌이 노래해요. (Aidol-i noraehaeyo.) - An idol sings. → 아이돌들이 노래해요. (Aidol-**deur**-i noraehaeyo.) - Idols sing.

While 들 **(deul)** is used to make nouns plural, it is important to note that Korean often relies on context rather than explicit plural markers. The use of 들 **(deul)** is more common in spoken language when the speaker wants to be clear about the plurality.

에 (e), 에서 (eseo), 부터 (buteo), and 까지 (kkaji): Location/Time Particles

Korean uses several particles to indicate location and time, which are equivalents of English prepositions. Here are the main location particles and their uses:

1. 에 (e)

Indicates the location where something exists (i.e. "in") or the direction toward which something is moving (i.e. "to"). 에 is also used to indicate time, similar to "at" in English.

Examples:

- 케이팝 아이돌들은 한국에 살아요 (Keipap aidoldeul-eun hanguk-**e** sarayo) - K-pop idols live in Korea.
- 학교에 가요. (Hakgyo-**e** gayo.) - (I) go to school.
- 콘서트는 저녁 8시에 시작해요 (Konseoteu-neun jeonyeok 8si-**e** sijakhaeyo.) - The concert starts at 8 p.m.

2. 에서 (eseo)

Indicates the location where an action is taking place (i.e. "in"). It can also mean "from" when indicating the starting point of an action.

Examples:

- 서울**에서** 출발해요. (Seoul-**eseo** chulbalhaeyo.) - (They) depart from Seoul.
- 연습실**에서** 춤춰요. (Yeonseupsil-**eseo** chumchwoyo.) - (I) dance in the practice room.

3. 부터 (buteo)

Indicates the starting point in time or space (i.e. "from").

Examples:

- 서울**부터** 부산까지 (Seoul-**buteo** Busankkaji) - From Seoul to Busan
- 아침**부터** 연습해요. (Achim-**buteo** yeonseuphaeyo.) - (They) practice from the morning.

4. 까지 (kkaji)

Indicates the endpoint in time or space (i.e. "up to/until").

Examples:

- 연습실**까지** 달려요. (Yeonseupsil-**kkaji** dallyeoyo.) - (They) run to the rehearsal room.
- 오후**까지** 연습해요. (Ohu-**kkaji** yeonseuphaeyo.) - (I) practice until the afternoon.

와, 과, 랑, 이랑, and 하고: Linking Particles

Linking particles in Korean are used to connect nouns together, similar to "and" in English. Here are the main linking particles and their uses:

와 (wa) / 과 (gwa)

1. **와 (wa):** Used after a noun ending in a vowel.
2. **과 (gwa):** Used after a noun ending in a consonant.

Examples:

- 블랙핑크**와** 트와이스 (Beullaekpingkeu-**wa** Teuwaiseu) - BLACKPINK and TWICE
- 앨범**과** 포토북 (aelbeom-**gwa** potobuk) - album and photobook

랑 / 이랑 (rang / irang)

1. **랑 (rang):** Used after a noun ending in a vowel.
2. **이랑 (irang):** Used after a noun ending in a consonant.

Examples:

- 콘서트랑 팬미팅 (konseoteu-**rang** paenmiting) - concert and fan meeting
- 아이돌이랑 팬 (aidol-**irang** paen) - idol and fan

The main difference between 와/과 and 랑/이랑 is that the former pair is more formal and used more in writing whereas the latter is more casual and more common in spoken Korean.

하고 (hago)

Can be used to connect two nouns and is neutral in formality, making it versatile for both casual and polite conversations. It is also used after any noun, regardless of whether it ends in a vowel or consonant.

Examples:

- 노래하고 춤 (norae-**hago** chum) - song and dance
- 멤버하고 스태프 (member-**hago** seutaepeu) - member and staff

의 (ui): Possessive Particles

The possessive particle, 의 (ui), is used to indicate possession, very similar to the apostrophe-s ('s) in English. When used in a sentence, the possessor comes first, followed by 의 (ui), then the possession.

Examples:

- 예지의 눈 (yeji-**ui** nun) - Yeji's eyes
- 가수의 목소리 (gaseu-**ui** moksori) - the singer's voice

While **의 (ui)** is more common in standard writing and formal speech, native speakers frequently change the pronunciation to **에 (e)** in casual conversation, particularly with certain pronouns. Similarly, in spoken Korean, 의 (ui) is often omitted when the context is clear.

For example, instead of saying 내 친구의 책 (nae chingu-ui chaek) for "my friend's book," people might just say 내 친구 책 (nae chingu chaek), "my friend book."

And in everyday speech you will hear:

- 나의(na-ui) → **내 (nae)** - "my" (informal)
- 저의(jeo-ui) → **제 (je)** - "my" (formal)
- 너의(neo-ui) → **네 (ne)** - "your" (informal)

Here is a list of "standard" possessive pronouns:

		Informal/Casual	Formal/Humble
First Person Singular	my	**나의** (na-ui)	**저의** (jeo-ui)
First Person Plural	our	**우리의** (uri-ui)	**저희의** (jeohui-ui)
Second Person Singular	your	**너의** (neo-ui)	**당신의** (dangsin-ui)*
Second Person Plural	your	**너희의** (neohui-ui)**	---***
Third Person Singular	his/her	**그의** (geu-ui)/**그녀의** (geunyeo-ui)****	
Third Person Plural	their	**그들의** (geudeul-ui)****	

*The polite second person singular, 당신의, is rarely used in conversations today. Instead, Korean speakers typically address others by their names or positions followed by the honorific suffix 님 (nim).

**The second person plural 너희 doesn't require a possessive particle. In other words, 너희 can mean both "you" and "your."

***For the polite second person plural, 여러분의 (yeoreobunui), meaning "everyone's," is most commonly used.

****그의, 그녀의, and 그들의 are literary words and practically never used in conversations. In most cases, the subject is implied; if clarification is necessary, Korean speakers will refer to a person by their name or say 그 분, meaning "that person" (polite).

도 (do): "Also" Particle

The particle 도 **(do)** is used to mean "also," "too," or "as well." It is used to indicate that the subject, object, or topic of the sentence shares the same characteristic or action as something previously mentioned.

도 **(do)** is attached directly to the noun or pronoun it modifies, replacing any subject, topic, or object particle — 이/가 **(i/ga),** 는/은 **(neun/eun),** or 를/을 **(reul/eul)** — that would normally be used.

Examples:

- 이 노래도 정말 좋아요. (I norae-**do** jeongmal joayo) - This song is also really good.
- 나도 투모로우바이투게더를 좋아해요. (na-**do** Tumorou-bai-tugedeo-reul joahaeyo) - I, too, like TXT.

만 (man): "Only" Particle

The particle 만 **(man)** is used to mean "only" or "just."

만 **(man)** is attached directly to the noun or pronoun it modifies. It emphasizes that the action or statement pertains exclusively to that noun or pronoun.

Examples:

- 그 사람은 춤**만** 잘 춰요. (Geu saram-eun chum-**man** jal chwoyo.) - He/She only dances well.
- 그 멤버는 노래**만** 불러요. (Geu maembeo-neun norae-**man** bulleoyo.) - That member only sings.

These are not the only particles in existence, but what we covered above should be enough to keep you busy for a while!

Pronoun + Particle Contraction: In Korean, pronouns and demonstrative pronouns such as "this," "that," "here," and "there" can contract with particles to make pronunciation more fluid and natural. These contractions simplify the language, making it more efficient for both spoken and written communication.

For example:

나 **(na)** - I, me (informal) and 저 **(jeo)** - I, me (formal)

- 나 + 가 **(ga)** → 내가 **(naega)** - I (as a subject)
- 저 + 가 **(ga)** → 제가 **(je-ga)** - I (as a subject)

and for

이것 **(igeot)** - this

58

- 이것 + 은 **(eun)** → 이건 **(igeon)** - this (as a topic)
- 이것 + 이 **(i)** → 이게 **(ige)** - this (as a subject)
- 이것 + 을 **(eul)** → 이걸 **(igeol)** - this (as an object)

Similarly, other pronouns and accompanying particles are contracted as seen in the following table.

Summary Table of Pronoun + Particle Contractions

Pronoun	English	Topic (는)	Subject (가)	Object (를)
저 (jeo)	I/me (formal)	저는 (jeoneun)	제가 (jega)	저를 (jeoreul)
나 (na)	I/me (informal)	나는 (naneun)	내가 (naega)	나를 (nareul)
너 (neo)	You/you (single)	너는 (neoneun)	네가 (nega)*	너를 (neoreul)
이것 (igeot)	This	이건 (igeon)	이게 (ige)	이걸 (igeol)
그것 (geugeot)	That	그건 (geugeon)	그게 (geuge)	그걸 (geugeol)
저것 (jeogeot)	That over there	저건 (jeogeon)	저게 (jeoge)	저걸 (jeogeol)

Although 네가 is the correct spelling of the word, it is more commonly pronounced as 니가 (niga) or 너가 (neoga) in conversations.

PUNCTUATION IN KOREAN

The Korean punctuation system has been influenced by European punctuation styles.

Punctuation Marks

The following are used commonly in Korean in the same way as they are in English:

1 . 마침표 (machimpyo)/Period - .

2. 쉼표 (swimpyo)/Comma - ,

3. 물음표 (mureumpyo)/Question mark - ?

4. 느낌표 (neukkimpyo)/Exclamation mark - !

5. 따옴표 (ttaompyo)/Quotation marks

- 큰따옴표 (keunttaompyo)/Double Quotation marks - " "
- 작은따옴표 (jageunttaompyo)/Single Quotation marks - ' '

6. 쌍점 (ssangjeom) / Colon - :

7. 쌍반점 (ssangbanjeom) / Semicolon - ;

8. 괄호 (gwalho) / Parentheses - **( )**

Spacing Between Words in Korean Writing

Korean uses spaces between words, similar to English, but there are specific rules about where to place spaces. Here are the key guidelines:

1. **Nouns and Particles:** Nouns, including pronouns, and their associated particles, such as topic markers, subject markers, object markers, etc., are bundled together and treated as one word.
2. **Predicates (linking verb + noun or adjective):** The "be verb" 이다 (ida) and its complements, which are nouns and adjectives, are written together. (We will cover this concept in the next chapter.)
3. **Compound Nouns:** Compound nouns, e.g., 콘서트장 (konseoteu-jang), are written together without spaces. (콘서트장 is a combination of 콘서트, "concert" written phonetically, and 장, a Sino-Korean word meaning "venue.")
4. **Numbers and Counters:** Numbers and counters are grouped together, but they are written with a space in between, e.g., 티켓 두 장 (tiket du jang). However, when the number is written with Arabic numerals, there is no space between the number and the counter, e.g., 티켓 2장 (tiket i-jang).

Example:

저는 뉴진스 팬이에요. 뉴진스 앨범 두 장 샀어요. (Jeoneun nyujinseu paen-ieyo. Nyujinseu aelbeom du jang sasseoyo.) - I'm a New Jeans fan. I bought two New Jeans' albums. / *I New Jeans fan am. (Subject omitted) New Jeans' new album two "jang" (counter for flat objects) bought.*

- 저는: The topic marker 는 (neun) is attached to the pronoun 저.
- 팬이에요: The verb 이다, conjugated into 이에요, is directly attached to the complement 팬.
- 두 장: The number 두 and the counter 장 are written with a space in between.

Now that we learned the basic sentence structure and commonly used particles, we can now delve deeper into one of the most crucial components of Korean grammar: verbs. In the next chapter, we will explore how verbs are conjugated and how they form the backbone of Korean sentences.

FIVE
VERBS & CONJUGATION
WHERE THE ACTION IS

VERBS ARE the backbone of sentences in any language, and Korean is no exception. They express actions, states, and emotions, making them essential for effective communication.

You've likely encountered various verbs already in song lyrics, interviews, and fan chants. Understanding how to conjugate and use Korean verbs will take your language skills to the next level. So let's dive right in!

THE BASICS

The infinitive form of Korean verbs ends with "다 (da)," and the part that precedes the "다" is called "verb stem." The underlined parts are the verb stems in the following examples:

- 하다(**ha**da): To do
- 노래**하**다 (norae-**ha**da); To sing
- 가다 (**ga**da): To go
- 먹다 (**meok**da): To eat
- 춤추다 (chum-**chu**da): To dance

All the conjugation takes place in the suffixes/endings you attach to these verb stems. You drop the "다" and replace it with the appropriate ending. Some of the rules can get a little tricky even for regular verbs. But overall, these rules are quite systematic, so if you take the time, you will be surprised how well you can learn them in a relatively short period of time.

Korean verbs do not conjugate according to gender or pronouns as verbs do in European languages. Instead, they primarily conjugate according to tense (future, present, past) and politeness levels (informal, polite, formal), based on hierarchical relationships between the speaker and the listener.

Whether the subject of the sentence is specified with a noun or pronoun or omitted/implied through context as they often are, it does *not* affect how the verb conjugates.

MORE ON THE ROLE OF HIERARCHY

The Korean language has a complex system of honorifics and politeness levels that are used to express respect; it indicates the speaker's relationship to the listener or the subject of the conversation. While this is a concept familiar to speakers of other Asian languages and some European languages, it may seem foreign to most English speakers.

The politeness level, verb endings, and vocabulary changes, depending on the relative social positions and intimacy between speakers. For example, when speaking to someone of a higher status or age, or to a stranger in a public place, Koreans use formal and polite language, employing honorific particles and special verb endings.

On the other hand, when speaking to someone of a lower status or younger age, or someone close to them like friends and family, Koreans may use more casual language. Failing to use the appropriate level of language can be considered rude, leading to potential misunderstandings or social *faux pas*.

Cultural side note: The hierarchy in Korean culture also extends to decision-making processes, seating arrangements, and gift-giving practices. In general, those who are higher in the hierarchy have more authority and influence in making decisions, and their opinions are given more weight. In social gatherings or meetings, seating arrangements often reflect the hierarchical order, with the most senior or highest-ranking individuals seated in positions of honor. In K-pop, you have probably noticed that members of the group are almost always listed or introduced in the order of age seniority — even when the difference may be a mere week or two.

POLITENESS LEVEL AND CONJUGATION

In Korean, politeness levels and conjugation are crucial for proper communication. The levels are generally categorized into informal, polite, and formal. Here is an overview of each level and ways to conjugate verbs accordingly.

반말 (Banmal) - Informal

- **Usage:** Used with close friends, family members of the same age, younger people, or in very casual situations. You hear idols talk among themselves in this form.
- **Characteristics:** Direct and simple, often ending in -아/어 (a/eo) for verbs.

존댓말 (Jondaemal) - Polite

- **Usage:** Used in everyday conversation with strangers, acquaintances, and in most social situations to show respect. You hear idols talk in this form in interviews and TV shows. This is the main form you should concentrate on as a beginner because it is the most versatile one and will help you avoid making social *faux pas*. Learn the various conjugations in this form, i.e., past polite, future polite, progressive polite, imperative polite, etc., then you can build on that foundation to learn other forms.
- **Characteristics:** Ends with -요 (yo) or other polite endings, indicating politeness.

Polite form involving the honorific 시 (si): The honorific 시 (si) is used to show respect or politeness towards the subject of the sentence. While politeness level varies depending on the endings such as -요 and -습니다 (-seumnida), 시 is an essential device that complements the -요 ending.

- **Usage:** 시 is added to the verb stem when the subject of the sentence is someone with higher status or elders (e.g. your grandmother or your company CEO). For example, 할머니가 요리하세요 (halmeoniga yorihaseyo) means "Grandma cooks." Here, the verb 요리하다 (yorihada) becomes 요리하시다 (yorihasida), which is then conjugated into 요리하세요

(yorihaseyo) in the present tense. When the subject of this sentence is 저 (jeo), however, the sentence becomes 저는 요리해요 (jeoneun yorihaeyo), meaning "I cook." Notice how the second example still reflects polite speech, as it ends with the polite ending -요.

- **Characteristics:** 시 is added to the verb stem and conjugated into the appropriate tense.

격식체 (Gyeoksikche) - Formal

- **Usage:** Used in formal situations such as presentations, official documents, speeches, interviews, and news reports. Also used when addressing someone of significantly higher status. You often hear idols talk to their fans using this form, reflecting their utmost respect and appreciation for you.
- **Characteristics:** Ends with -ㅂ니다/습니다 (mnida/seumnida)* for verbs, indicating high respect and formality. *Example of consonant assimilation (ㅂ → ㅁ)*

REGULAR VS. IRREGULAR VERB CONJUGATION

Like many other languages, Korean verbs can be categorized into regular and irregular verbs based on their conjugation patterns. Regular verbs follow predictable conjugation rules, making them easier to learn and use. On the other hand, irregular verbs have unique conjugation patterns that just need to be memorized.

To conjugate regular verbs, remove the final syllable 다 (da) and replace it with the appropriate verb ending. For example, for 만나다 (mannada), "to meet (someone)," the conjugation looks like this:

- 만나요 (manna-yo) - (We) meet (polite, present tense)
- 만났어요 (manna-sseoyo) - (We) met (polite, past tense)
- 만날 거예요 (mannal-geoyeyo) - (We) will meet (polite, future tense)

Notice how the stem, 만나, remains unchanged? What follows are endings used for conjugation, and although there are many more of them (for different politeness levels, for instance), they remain more or less the same for all regular verbs. In other words, if you memorize them, you will be able to conjugate the vast majority of Korean verbs!

Irregular verbs, however, have stems that change when conjugated, requiring special attention. We will go over them later.

But first, we will concentrate on regular verb conjugation, going over the ground rules and some examples.

REGULAR VERB CONJUGATION

The first step in conjugating regular verbs is to *identify the last vowel of the verb stem*. So drop the last 다, then take a close look at the last syllable of the remaining verb stem, and find the last vowel in it.

Examples:

- In 먹다 (meok-da), "to eat," the vowel in the last syllable of the stem, 먹, is ㅓ
- In 마시다 (masi-da), "to drink," the vowel in the last syllable of the stem, 시, is ㅣ
- In 놀다 (nol-da), "to play," the vowel in the last syllable of the stem, 놀, is ㅗ
- In 만나다 (manna-da), "to meet," the vowel in the last syllable of the stem, 나, is ㅏ

A spotlight (조명, jomyeong) on 하다 (hada): The verb 하다 (hada), which means "to do," is one of the most important and versatile verbs in the Korean language.

While 하다 functions as a base verb on its own, it is largely used in combination with nouns to form a vast array of compound verbs.

For example, to form the verb "to sing", you combine the noun for "song," 노래 (norae), and the verb "to do", 하다 (hada), to make 노래하다 (noraehada). Other examples of compound "hada verbs" include:

- 공부 (gongbu), "studies" + 하다 → 공부하다 (gongbuhada), "to study"
- 말 (mal), "speech" + 하다 → 말하다 (malhada) "to speak"
- 요리 (yori) "cuisine/dish" + 하다 → 요리하다 (yorihada) "to cook"
- 랩 (raep), "rap" + 하다 → 랩하다 (raephada) "to rap"

All of these 하다 verbs follow the same rules. 하다 is a regular verb that follows the conjugation rules for stems ending with 아, but it requires minor tweaking as you will see soon. Once you master 하다 conjugations, you will be able to conjugate about 57% of all Korean verbs. Just like that!

Now, without further ado, let's start conjugating some verbs. Again, remember that Korean verbs conjugate according to politeness levels and tenses only; it doesn't matter who or how many people are performing the action. Unlike in some languages, Korean verbs don't change based on the subject's person (first, second, or third) or number (singular or plural).

현재 시제 (hyeonjae sije)/Present Tense

To conjugate regular verbs for the present tense, simply add the following endings to the verb stem according to the last vowel in the stem:

Last Vowel	Informal	Polite	Polite with -시 (si)	Formal
ㅏ or ㅗ	-아 (-a)	-아요 (-ayo)	Stem ending with a -Vowel: -세요 (-seyo) -Consonant: -으세요 (-euseyo)	Stem ending with a -Vowel: -ㅂ니다 (-mnida) -Consonant: -습니다 (-seumnida)
Others	-어 (-eo)	-어요 (-eoyo)		

Note on vowel assimilation: If the verb stem ends with a vowel, 아 or 어 of the endings get combined with the previous syllable. Here is how it works:

Vowel + Vowel Combination	Example
ㅏ + 아 (a + a) → ㅏ (a)	가다 (to go), 가 + 아 (ga + a) → 가 (ga)
ㅗ + 아 (o + a) → ㅘ (wa)	보다 (to see), 보+아 (bo + a) → 봐 (bwa)
ㅓ + 어 (eo + eo) → ㅓ (eo)	서다 (to stand), 서 + 어 (seo + eo) → 서 (seo)
ㅣ + 어 (i + eo) → ㅕ (yeo)	마시다 (to drink), 마시 + 어 (masi + eo) → 마셔 (masyeo)
ㅜ + 어 (eu + eo) → ㅝ (wo)	춤추다 (to dance), 춤추 + 어 (chumchu +eo) → 춤춰 (chumchwo)

Throughout this conjugation section, we will use these three verbs as examples: 가다 (gada), "to go"; 하다 (hada), "to do"; 먹다 (meokda), "to eat." (The 하다 anomalies are lightly shaded below.)

Verb	Informal	Polite	Polite with -시 (si)	Formal
가다	가 (ga)	가요 (gayo)	가세요 (gaseyo)	갑니다 (gamnida)
하다	해 (hae)	해요 (haeyo)	하세요 (haseyo)	합니다 (hamnida)
먹다	먹어 (meogeo)	먹어요 (meogeoyo)	드세요* (deuseyo)	먹습니다 (meokseumnida)

Some Korean verbs have two distinct words for informal and polite speech. Common examples include 먹다 (meokda) / 드시다 (dusida), "to eat"; 자다 (jada) / 주무시다 (jumusida), "to sleep"; 있다 (itda) / 계시다 (gyesida), "to be or to stay."

Examples (polite form):

- 학교에 가요. (Hakgyoe gayo.) - (I) go to school.
- 숙제를 해요. (Sukjereul haeyo.) - (I) do homework.
- 밥을 먹어요. (Bapeul meogeoyo.) - (I) eat rice.

과거 시제 (gwageo sije)/Past Tense

To conjugate regular verbs for the present tense, simply add the following endings to the verb stem according to the last vowel in the stem:

Last Vowel	Informal	Polite	Polite with -시 (si)	Formal
ㅏ or ㅗ	-았어 (-asseo)	-았어요 (-asseoyo)	-셨어요 (-syeosseoyo)	-았습니다 (-asseumnida)
Others	-었어 (-eosseo)	-었어요 (-eosseoyo)		-었습니다 (-eosseumnida)

For our three representative verbs, it looks like this:

Verb	Informal	Polite	Polite with -시 (si)	Formal
가다	갔어 (gasseo)	갔어요 (gasseoyo)	가셨어요 (gasyeosseoyo)	갔습니다 (gasseumnida)
하다	했어 (haesseo)	했어요 (haesseoyo)	하셨어요 (hasyeosseoyo)	했습니다 (haesseumnida)
먹다	먹었어 (meogeosseo)	먹었이요 (meogeosseoyo)	드셨어요 (deusyeosseoyo)	먹었습니나 (meogeosseumnida)

Examples (polite form):

- 저는* 학교에 갔어요. (Jeoneun hakgyoe gasseoyo.) - I went to school.

- 저는 숙제를 했어요. (Jeoneun sukjereul haesseoyo.) - I did my homework.
- 저는 밥을 먹었어요. (Jeoneun bapeul meogeosseoyo.) - I ate (my meal, or literally "rice").

저는 (subject + topic particle) can be omitted. Often, it sounds better when the subject is omitted/implied.

미래 시제 (mirae sije)/Future Tense

For the future tense, look to see if the verb stem ends in a vowel or a consonant, and add the following endings to the verb stem:

Stem Ending	Informal	Polite	Polite with -시 (si)	Formal
Vowel	-ㄹ 거야 (-l geoya)	-ㄹ 거예요 (-l geoyeyo)	-실 거예요 (-sil geoyeyo)	-ㄹ 겁니다 (-l geomnida)
Consonant	-을 거야 (-eul geoya)	-을 거예요 (-eul geoyeyo)	-으실 거예요 (-eusil geoyeyo)	-을 겁니다 (eul-geomnida)

For our three representative verbs, it looks like this:

Verb	Informal	Polite	Polite with -시 (si)	Formal
가다	갈 거야 (gal geoya)	갈 거예요 (gal geoyeyo)	가실 거예요 (gasil geoyeyo)	갈 것입니다 (gal geosimnida)
하다	할 거야 (hal geoya)	할 거예요 (hal geoyeyo)	하실 거예요 (hasil geoyeyo)	할 것입니다 (hal geosimnida)
먹다	먹을 거야 (meogeul geoya)	먹을 거예요 (meogeul geoyeyo)	드실 거예요 (deusil geoyeyo)	먹을 것입니다 (meogeul geosimnida)

Examples (polite form):

- 저는 학교에 갈 거예요. (Jeoneun hakgyoe gal geoyeyo.) - I will go to school.
- 저는 숙제를 할 거예요. (Jeoneun sukjereul hal geoyeyo.) - I will do my homework.
- 저는 밥을 먹을 거예요. (Jeoneun bapeul meogeul geoyeyo.) - I will eat (my meal).

현재진행형 (hyeonjaejinhaenghyeong)/Present Progressive (be ~ing)

Present Progressive (or Continuous) form expresses an action that is currently going on. It is the easiest to conjugate. Just add the following to the verb stem:

Informal	Polite	Polite with -시 (si)	Formal
-고 있어 (-go isseo)	-고 있어요 (-go isseoyo)	-시고 계세요 (-sigo gyeseyo)	-고 있습니다 (-go itseumnida)

This one is super straight forward:

Verb	Informal	Polite	Polite with -시 (si)	Formal
가다	가고 있어 (gago isseo)	가고 있어요 (gago isseoyo)	가시고 계세요 (gasigo gyeseyo)	가고 있습니다 (gago itseumnida)
하다	하고 있어 (hago isseo)	하고 있어요 (hago isseoyo)	하시고 계세요 (hasigo gyeseyo)	하고 있습니다 (hago itseumnida)
먹다	먹고 있어 (meokgo isseo)	먹고 있어요 (meokgo isseoyo)	드시고 계세요 (deusigo gyeseyo)	먹고 있습니다 (meokgo itseumnida)

Examples (polite form):

- 저는 학교에 가고 있어요. (Jeoneun hakgyoe gago isseoyo.) - I am going to school.
- 저는 숙제를 하고 있어요. (Jeoneun sukjereul hago isseoyo.) - I am doing my homework.
- 저는 밥을 먹고 있어요. (Jeoneun bapeul meokgo isseoyo.) - I am eating (my meal.)

명령형 (myeongnyeonghyeong)/Imperative Form (Do it!)

Imperative forms are used to express commands such as "Sing!" or "Run!"

For imperatives, simply add the following endings to the verb stem according to the last vowel in the stem:

Last Vowel	Informal	Polite	Polite with -시 (si)	Formal
ㅏ or ㅗ	-아 (-a)	-아요 (-ayo)	Either way, stem ending with a -Vowel: -세요 (-seyo) -Consonant: -으세요 (-euseyo)	Either way, stem ending with a -Vowel: -십시오 (-sipsio) -Consonant: -으십시오 (-eusipsio)
Others	-어 (-eo)	-어요 (-eoyo)		

For our three representative verbs, it looks like this:

Verb	Informal	Polite	Polite with Honorific -시 (si)	Formal
가다	가 (ga)	가요 (gayo)	가세요 (gaseyo)	가십시오 (gasipsio)
하다	해 (hae)	하세요 (haseyo)	하세요 (haseyo)	하십시오 (hasipsio)
먹다	먹어 (meogeo)	먹어요 (meogeoyo)	드세요 (deuseyo)	드십시오 (deusipsio)*

Examples (polite form):

- 학교에 가세요 (hakgyoe gaseyo) - Go to school.
- 숙제를 하세요 (sukjereul haseyo) - Do your homework.
- 밥/진지* 드세요 (bap/jinji deuseyo) - Eat (your meal).

*진지 (jinji) is a polite word for 밥 (bap), meaning "meal or a bowl of cooked rice." 진지 is reserved for elderly members of your family.

청유형 (cheongyuhyeong)/Propositive (Let's ~!)

Propositive forms are used to express suggestions and requests. To conjugate, simply add the following endings to the verb stem according to the last vowel in the stem:

Last Vowel	Informal	Polite	Formal
ㅏ or ㅗ	-자 (-ja)	-요 (-yo)	Either way, stem ending with a -Vowel: -ㅂ시다 (-psida)
Others		-어요 (-eoyo)	-Consonant: -읍시다 (-eupsida)

For our usual examples:

Verb	Informal	Polite	Formal
가다	가자 (gaja)	가요 (gayo)	갑시다 (gapsida)
하다	하자 (haja)	해요 (haeyo)	합시다 (hapsida)
먹다	먹자 (meokja)	먹어요 (meogeoyo)	먹읍시다 (meogeupsida)

Examples (polite form):

- 학교에 가요! (hakgyoe gayo) - Let's go to school!
- 숙제를 해요! (sukjereul haeyo) - Let's do homework!
- 밥을 먹어요! (bapeul meogeoyo) - Let's eat!

Here is your all-in-one conjugation cheatsheet for regular verbs:

Summary Table of Regular Verb Conjugation

Tense	Informal	Polite	Polite with -시 (si)	Formal
Present	-아 / 어 (a/eo)	-아요 / 어요 (ayo/eoyo)	-세요 / 으세요 (seyo/euseyo)	-ㅂ니다 / 습니다 (-mnida/seumnida)
Past	-았어/ 었어 (asseo/eosseo)	-았어요 / 었어요 (asseoyo/ eosseoyo)	-셨어요 (syeosseoyo)	-았습니다 / 었습니다 (asseumnida/ eosseumnida)
Future	-ㄹ 거야 / 을 거야 (l geoya/ eul geoya)	-ㄹ 거예요 / 을 거예요 (l geoyeyo/ eul geoyeyo)	-실 거예요 / 으실 거예요 (sil geoyeyo/ eusil geoyeyo)	-ㄹ 겁니다 / 을 겁니다 (l geomnida/ eul geomnida)
Progressive	-고 있어 (go isseo)	-고 있어요 (go isseoyo)	-시고 계세요 (sigo gyeseyo)	-고 있습니다 (go itseumnida)
Imperative	-아 / 어 (a/eo)	-아요 / 어요 (ayo/eoyo)	-세요 / 으세요 (seyo/euseyo)	-십시오 / 으십시오 (-sipsio/eusipsio)
Propositive	-자 (-ja)	-요 / 어요 (yo/eoyo)	---	-ㅂ시다 / 읍시다 (psida/eupsida)

A spotlight (조명) on 이다 (ida) and 있다 (itda): Korean does have verbs that can function similarly to the English verb "to be," but they are used differently and are context-specific. 이다 (ida) and 있다 (itda) are the two main Korean verbs for "to be" — both regular verbs. Here's the breakdown:

이다 (ida)

Usage: Used to identify someone/something or describe a permanent or fundamental quality of someone/something. 이다 is associated with the question "what is it?" The ending you use depends on whether the preceding noun ends with a consonant or a vowel.

Example:

- 나는 케이팝 팬**이야**. (Naneun keipap paen-iya.) - I am a K-pop fan. (Informal)
- 저는 케이팝 팬**이에요**. (Jeoneun keipap paen-ieyo.) - I am a K-pop fan. (Polite)
- 저는 케이팝 팬입니다. (Jeoneun keipap paen-imnida.) - I am a K-pop fan. (Formal)
- 이건* 뮤직비디오**야**. (Igeon myujikbidio-ya.) - This is a music video. (Informal)

- 이건 뮤직비디오**예요.** (Igeon myujikbidio-yeyo.) - This is a music video. (Polite)
- 이건 뮤직비디오**입니다.** (Igeon myujikbidio-imnida.) - This is a music video. (Formal)

이건 (igeon) is a shortened version of 이것은 (igeos-eun); the former is more commonly used. The latter is a demonstrative pronoun with a topic particle.

이다, "to be," is a linking verb, which connect the subject with a noun or an adjective. There are no Present Progressive, Imperative, or Propositive forms. Below is all you need to know:

Tense	Informal	Polite	Polite with -시 (si)	Formal
Present	Noun ending w/ Consonant: 이야 (iya) Vowel: 야 (ya)	Noun ending w/ C: 이에요 (ieyo) V: 예요 (yeyo)	Noun ending w/ C: 이세요 (iseyo) V: 세요 (seyo)	입니다 (imnida)
Past	Noun ending w/ C: 이었어 (ieosseo) V: 였어 (yeosseo)	Noun ending w/ C: 이었어요 (ieosseoyo) V: 였어요 (yeosseoyo)	Noun ending w/ C: 이셨어요 (isyeosseoyo) V: 셨어요 (syeosseoyo)	Noun ending w/ C: 이었습니다 (ieosseumnida) V: 였습니다 (yeosseumnida)
Future	일 거야 (il geoya)	일 거예요 (il geoyeyo)	Noun ending w/ C: 이실 거예요 (isil geoyeyo) V: 실 거예요 (sil geoyeyo)	일 것입니다 (il geosimnida)

있다 (itda)

Usage: Used to indicate existence or presence. It is associated with the question "where is it?" 있다 can also mean "to have." (The English verb "to have" does not translate well into Korean.)

Example:

- 나 집에 **있어.** (Na jibe isseo) - I am at home / "I exist at home". (Informal)
- 저는 집에 **있어요.** (Jeo-neun jibe isseoyo) - I am at home. (Polite)
- 저는 집에 **있습니다.** (Jeo-neun jibe itseumnida) - I am at home. (Formal)
- 그는 누나가 **있어.** (Geu-neun nuna-ga isseo) - He has an older sister / "An older sister exists for him". (Informal)

- 그는 누나가 **있어요**. (Geu-neun nuna-ga isseoyo) -He has an older sister. (Polite)
- 그는 누나가 **있습니다**. (Geu-neun nuna-ga itseumnida) - He has an older sister. (Formal)

있다 is considered a regular verb, but like 하다, it is such an important verb, so its conjugation deserves its own spotlight:

Tense	Informal	Polite	Polite with -시 (si)	Formal
Present	있어 (isseo)	있어요 (isseoyo)	계세요 (gyeseyo)	있습니다 (itseumnida)
Past	있었어 (isseosseo)	있었어요 (isseosseoyo)	계셨어요 (gyesyeosseoyo)	있었습니다 (isseotseumnida)
Future	있을 거야 (isseul geoya)	있을 거예요 (isseul geoyeyo)	계실 거예요 (gyesil geoyeyo)	있을 것입니다 (isseul geosimnida)
Progressive	있고 있어 (itgo isseo)	있고 있어요 (itgo isseoyo)	---	---
Imperative	있어 (isseo)	있어 (isseo)	계세요 (gyeseyo)	---
Propositive	있자 (itja)	있어요 (isseoyo)		---

IRREGULAR VERB CONJUGATION

In Korean, several types of irregular verb conjugation patterns occur. These irregularities typically happen in the final consonant of the verb stem when it is followed by a vowel ending. While it is not necessary to master all of them, it helps to know that they exist. Here are the main types of irregular verb conjugation patterns:

1. ㅅ Irregular Verbs (ㅅ 불규칙 동사)

- When the final consonant of the verb stem is ㅅ, it often disappears before a vowel.
- **Example:** 붓다 (to pour) becomes 부어요 (bueoyo) in the present tense.

2. ㄷ Irregular Verbs (ㄷ 불규칙 동사)

- When the final consonant of the verb stem is ㄷ, it changes to ㄹ before a vowel.
- **Example:** 듣다 (to listen) becomes 들어요 (deureoyo) in the present tense.

3. ㅂ Irregular Verbs (ㅂ 불규칙 동사)

- When the final consonant of the verb stem is ㅂ, it changes to 오 or 우 before a vowel.
- **Example:** 돕다 (to help) becomes 도와요 (dowayo) in the present tense.

4. ㅡ Irregular Verbs (ㅡ 불규칙 동사)

- When the verb stem ends in ㅡ, the ㅡ is dropped, and the preceding vowel determines the conjugation.
- **Example:** 잠그다 (to lock), becomes 잠가요 (jamgayo) in the present tense.

5. 르 Irregular Verbs (르 불규칙 동사)

- When the verb stem ends in 르, an additional ㄹ is added, and 르 changes to 라 or 러 before a vowel.
- **Example:** 자르다, (to cut) becomes 잘라요 (jallayo) in the present tense.

COMMON MODAL VERBS

"Modal verbs" are those words you can use to modify verbs to express abilities, possibilities, permissions, obligations, and other related concepts in English, such as "can," "may," "must," and "should." Here are the counterparts in Korean:

1. 할 수 있다 (hal su itda) - Can

This phrase means "can" or "to be able to," indicating ability or possibility. 할 수 있다 literally means "to do-ability-exists."

Structure:

- Verb stem + -을 수 있다 (-eul su itda) — if the verb stem ends in a consonant
- Verb stem + -ㄹ 수 있다 (-l su itda) — if the verb stem ends in a vowel
- For all 하다 (hada) verbs, replace 하다 with 할 수 있다 (hal su itda)

Examples:

- 한국어를 읽**을 수 있어요.** (Hangugeo-reul ilg**eul su isseoyo.**) — (I) can read Korean.
- 내일 만날 **수 있어요.** (Naeil manna-**l su isseoyo.**) — (I) can meet tomorrow.
- 노래**할 수 있어요.** (Norae**hal su isseoyo.**) — (I) can sing.

2. 해도 되다 (haedo doeda) - May

This phrase is used to ask for or give permission, similar to "may" in English. 되다 means "to become" or "to be allowed."

Structure:

- Verb stem + **-아도 되다** (-ado doeda) — if the last vowel of the verb stem is ㅏ or ㅗ.
- Verb stem + **-어도 되다** (-eodo doeda) — if the last vowel of the verb stem is any other vowel
- Verb stem + **-여도 되다** (-aedo doeda) — if the verb stem ends with 하. This becomes 해도 되다 (haedo doeda) due to contraction, and all 하다 verbs follow this pattern.

되다 **(doeda)** is a verb meaning "to become" or "to be allowed." You need to know how to conjugate it in order to use it in sentences. It is an irregular verb that follows the following set of rules:

Tense	Informal	Polite	Formal
Present	돼 (dwae)	돼요 (dwaeyo)	됩니다 (doemnida)
Past	됐어 (dwaesseo)	됐어요 (dwaesseoyo)	됐습니다 (dwaesseumnida)
Future	될 거야 (doel geoya)	될 거예요 (doel geoyeyo)	될 것입니다 (doel geosimnida)
Progressive	---	---	---
Imperative	돼 (dwae)	되세요 (doeseyo)	되십시오 (doesipsio)
Propositive	---	---	---

Examples (in polite form):

- 지금 가도 **돼요.** (Jigeum g**ado dwaeyo.**) — You may go now.

- 여기서 먹**어도 돼**요. (Yeogiseo meog-**eodo dwaeyo**.) — You may eat here.
- 여기서 연습**해도 돼**요? (Yeogiseo yeonseup-**haedo dwaeyo?**) — May I practice here?

3. 해야 하다 / 해야 되다 (haeya hada / haeya doeda) - Must

To express obligation or responsibility, like in "must" or "have to" in English, you use the construction -아/어/여야 하다 or -아/어/여야 되다. Both forms are commonly used and can often be interchangeable.

Structure:

- Verb stem + **-아야 하다/되다** (-aya hada/doeda) — if the last vowel of the verb stem is ㅏ or ㅗ.
- Verb stem + **-어야 하다/되다** (-eoya hada/doeda) — if the last vowel of the verb stem any other vowel.
- Verb stem + **-여야 하다/되다** (-eoya hada/doeda) — if the verb stem ends with 하. This becomes **해야 하다/되다** (-haeya hada/doeda) due to contraction, and all 하다 verbs follow this pattern.

Examples (polite form):

- 지금 가야 해요. (Jigeum g**aya haeyo**.) - (I) must go now.
- 지금 가야 돼요. (Jigeum g**aya dwaeyo**.) - (I) have to go now.
- 아침을 먹어야 해요. (Achim-eul meog-**eoya haeyo**.) - (I) must eat breakfast.
- 아침을 먹어야 돼요. (Achim-eul meog-**eoya dwaeyo**.) - (I) have to eat breakfast.
- 숙제를 해야 해요. (Sukjereul **haeya haeyo**.) - (I) must do my homework.
- 숙제를 해야 돼요. (Sukjereul **haeya dwaeyo**.) - (I) have to do my homework.

Note that the -아/어/여야 하다 form can also be used to express "should" or strong recommendation, depending on the context.

(See Appendix for a list of essential verbs.)

Mastering verb conjugation takes time and practice, but with consistent effort, you will soon find yourself using these verbs to connect with others in the K-pop community.

SIX
ADJECTIVES & ADVERBS
THE BLING

JUST AS VERBS are essential for expressing actions, adjectives play a crucial role in describing people, places, and things — in *any* language, including Korean. Adverbs also convey intensity and texture to otherwise bland descriptions of actions by telling us *how* someone is doing something. Both adjectives and adverbs add depth and nuance, allowing you to express yourself more vividly.

In the world of K-pop, adjectives are particularly important for describing the unique qualities of your favorite idols or conveying the emotions evoked by a powerful performance. Whether you are gushing about your bias's stunning look or describing songs from the newest release, mastering Korean adjectives is key to successful communication.

This chapter will cover the basics of how to use adjectives and adverbs in Korean sentences and their conjugation patterns.

형용사 (HYEONGYONGSA) - ADJECTIVES

Adjectives describe the qualities or states of nouns as you probably already know. You may not have thought about it this way, but even in English, adjectives are used in two different ways, and the same holds true for Korean:

1. The K-drama star **is handsome.** - K-드라마 스타는 **잘생겼어요.** (K-deurama seutaneun **jalsaenggyeosseoyo.**)
2. The **handsome** man is a K-drama star. - **잘생긴** 남자는 K-드라마 스타예요. (**Jalsaenggin** namjaneun K-deurama seutayeyo.)

In the first example, the adjective "handsome," together with the preceding "is," come at the end of the sentence, acting like a verb. Words that function like verbs are called "**predicates**" (or descriptive verbs); so "is handsome" is a predicate. Unlike in English, verb-like adjectives are conjugated just like verbs in Korean — as you might have noticed in the example.

In the second sentence, the same adjective "handsome" simply modifies/describes the noun that follows, i.e., "man." These are called "**attributive adjectives**," and while we don't conjugate them like verbs, we do modify them.

Basic Structure

Korean adjectives typically end in **-다 (-da)** in their base form (or "dictionary form"), just like the infinitives of verbs.

Examples of Common Adjectives:

- 작다 **(jakda)** - to be small
- 크다 **(keuda)** - to be big
- 예쁘다 **(yeppeuda)** - to be pretty
- 빠르다 **(ppareuda)** - to be fast
- 느리다 **(neurida)** - to be slow

When used as predicates, they must be conjugated according to the tense and formality of the sentence — just like verbs. And just as with verbs, you first remove the 다 and add the proper endings to the stem. For attributive adjectives — the ones that come before nouns, you take the same stem and add ㄴ (n) or 은 (eun).

Regular Conjugation of Predicates (Linking Verb + Adjective):

Again, just like verbs, there are regular adjectives that follow predictable rules, and irregular adjectives that veer off the path a little bit. But the great news is, the regular adjective conjugation rules are almost exactly the same as the ones for regular verbs.

Compare the table below to the Summary Table of Regular Verb Conjugation in the last chapter (p.72 in print books):

Tense	Informal	Polite	Formal
Present	**-아 /어** (a/eo)	**-아요/어요** (ayo/eoyo)	**-ㅂ니다 /습니다** (-mnida/seumnida)
Past	**-았어/었어** (asseo/eosseo)	**-았어요/었어요** (asseoyo/eosseoyo)	**-았습니다/었습니다** (asseumnida/eosseumnida)
Future	**-ㄹ 거야/을 거야** (I geoya/eul geoya)	**-ㄹ 거예요/을 거예요** (I geoyeyo/eul geoyeyo)	**-ㄹ 겁니다/을 겁니다** (I geomnida/eul geomnida)
Progressive	**-고 있어** (go isseo)	**-고 있어요** (go isseoyo)	**-고 있습니다** (go itseumnida)
Imperative	**-아 /어** (a/eo)	**-아요/어요** (ayo/eoyo)	**-아십시오/어십시오** (-asipsio/eosipsio)
Propositive	**-자** (-ja)	**-요/어요** (yo/eoyo)	**-ㅂ시다/읍시다** (psida/eupsida)

Irregular Adjectives for Predicates:

Some adjectives are "irregular" and have their own rules based on their stem endings. Here are some to look out for:

1. ㅂ Irregular

When the stem ends in ㅂ, it changes to 우 before a vowel.

-가깝다 **(gakkapda) - to be close**

- Present: 가까워요 (gakkaweoyo)
- Past: 가까웠어요 (gakkaweosseoyo)
- Future: 가까울 거예요 (gakkaul geoyeyo)

2. ㅅ Irregular

When the stem ends in ㅅ, the ㅅ is dropped before certain endings..

-낫다 **(natda) - to be better**

- Present: 나아요 (na-ayo)
- Past: 나았어요 (na-asseoyo)
- Future: 나을 거예요 (naeul geoyeyo)

3. 르 Irregular

When the verb stem ends in 르, an additional ㄹ is added, and 르 changes to 라 or 러 before a vowel.

-다르다 **(dareuda) - to be different**

- Present: 달라요 (dallayo)
- Past: 달랐어요 (dallasseoyo)
- Future: 다를 거예요 (dareul geoyeyo)

Attributive/Descriptive Adjective Form

As mentioned, when an adjective precedes a noun, it takes on an attributive form. This form varies, once again, based on the stem ending of the adjective.

General Rules:

1. Stem Ending in a Vowel — For adjectives whose stem ends in a vowel, add - ㄴ (n).

Example A: 느리다 (neurida) - to be slow

- Stem: 느리 (neuri)
- Attributive Form: 느린 (neuri-**n**)
- Usage Example: 느린 자동차 (neuri**n** jadongcha) - slow car

Example B: 특별하다 (teukbyeolhada) - to be special (and all other 하다 adjectives)

- Stem: 특별하 (teukbyeolha)
- Attributive Form: 특별한 (teukbyeolha-**n**)
- Usage Example: 특별한 공연 (teukbyeolha**n** gongyeon) - a special performance / show

2. Stem Ending in a Consonant — For adjectives whose stem ends in a consonant, you add -은 (-eun).

Example: 작다 **(jakda)** - to be small

- Stem: 작 (jak)
- Attributive Form: 작은 (jag-**eun**)
- Usage Example: 작은 방 (jag-**eun** bang) - small room

Irregular Attributive Adjectives:

1. ㅂ Irregular: — When the stem ends in ㅂ, it changes to 운.

Example: 귀엽다 (gwiyeopda) - to be cute

- Stem: 귀엽 (gwiyeop)

- Attributive Form: 귀여운 (gwiyeo**un**)
- Usage Example: 귀여운 의상 (gwiyeo**un** uisang) - cute costume

2. ㄹ Irregular — When the stem ends in ㄹ, the ㄹ is dropped, and ㄴ is added.

Example: 길다 **(gilda)** - to be long

- Stem: 길 (gil)
- Attributive Form: 긴 (gi**n**)
- Usage Example: 긴 머리 (gi**n** meori) - long hair

3. ㅎ Irregular — When the stem ends in ㅎ, the ㅎ is dropped, and ㄴ is added.

Example: 빨갛다 **(ppalgata)** - to be red

- Stem: 빨갛 (ppalgat)
- Attributive Form: 빨간 (ppalga**n**)
- Usage Example: 빨간 얼굴 (ppalga**n** eolgul) - a red face

To summarize:

Base Form	Meaning	Stem Ending	Attributive Form
느리다 (neurida)	to be slow	vowel	느린 (neuri-n)
작다 (jakda)	to be small	consonant	작은 (jag-eun)
귀엽다 (gwiyeopda)	to be cute	consonant ㅂ	귀여운 (gwiyeoun)
길다 (gilda)	to be long	consonant ㄹ	긴 (gin)
빨갛다 (bbalgata)	to be red	consonant ㅎ	빨간 (bbalgan)

부사 (BUSA) - ADVERBS

Adverbs in Korean modify verbs, adjectives, or other adverbs, providing more information about how, when, where, or to what degree something happens.

Formation of Adverbs

Adverbs are formed by a couple of simple rules:

히 (hi) Adverbs: If the adjective you are trying to turn into an adverb is a 하다 adjective, simply replace the 하다 with 히 (hi).

Example: 조용하다 (joyonghada) — to be quiet

- Adverb: 조용히 (joyong**hi**) — quietly
- Usage Example: 조용히 웃었어요. (joyong**hi** useosseoyo.) — (subject omitted) quietly smiled.

게 (ge) Adverbs: For other adjectives, form adverbs by adding **-게 (ge)** to the stem of the adjective — similar to how you would attach "-ly" to a lot of English adjectives to form adverbs.

Example: 아름답다 (areumdapda) - beautiful

- Adverb: 아름답게 (areumdap-**ge**) — beautifully
- Usage Example: 아름답게 노래해요. (Areumdap**ge** noraehaeyo.) — (subject omitted) sings beautifully.

(Note that in Korean, the adverb always comes before the verb, while in English, an adverb can come before or after the verb.)

Degree Adverbs

Then, there are other special adverbs that are not formed from adjectives. The following adverbs modify adjectives and other adverbs to convey the intensity or degree to which they describe an action, state, or quality.

1. 매우 (mae-u) and 아주 (aju) — very; 매우 is slightly more literary than 아주

Examples:

- 노래를 **매우** 잘 불러요. (Noraereul **maeu** jal bulleoyo) - (subject omitted) sings very well.
- 그 사람은 일을 **아주** 열심히 해요. (Geu saram-eun ireul **aju** yeolsimhi haeyo) - He/She works very hard.

2. 정말 (jeongmal) and 진짜 (jinjja) — really / truly; 진짜 (jinjja) is extremely commonly used as it is versatile and expressive, like "really" in English.

Examples:

- 너 **정말** 많이 먹었어. (Neo **jeongmal** mani meogeosseo) - You really ate a lot.
- 기차가 **진짜** 빨라요. (Gichaga **jinjja** ppallayo) - The train is really fast.

3. 너무 (neomu) — too, very

Example:

- **너무** 늦었어요. (**Neomu** neujeosseo) - (We) were too late.

4. 꽤 (kkwae) — quite, fairly

Example:

- 그 사람은 노래를 **꽤** 잘해요. (Geu saram-eun noraereul **kkwae** jalhaeyo) - He / She sings pretty well.

5. 조금 (jogeum) /좀 (jom)* — a little, somewhat; *좀 is a shortened version of 조금.

Example:

- 이거 **좀** 도와줄래? (Igeo **jom** dowajullae?) - Can you help me a little?

6. 더 (deo) — more

Example:

- **더** 발전된 (**deo** baljeondoen) — more advanced

7. 가장 (gajang) and 제일 (jeil) — most; 가장 (gajang) is a little more formal and literary than 제일 (jeil)

Examples:

- **가장** 재능 있는 (**gajang** jaeneung inneun) — most talented

84

- 제일 빠른 (**jeil** ppareun) - fastest

(We will cover comparative and superlative sentences more in depth in the next chapter.)

Adjectives and adverbs are powerful tools in conversations. Mastering Korean adjectives and adverbs will enable you to construct more complex and precise sentences.

(See Appendix for more helpful adjectives and adverbs.)

SEVEN
MORE SENTENCE STRUCTURES
NEGATIONS & QUESTIONS

GUESS WHAT? You already know enough to string together simple, affirmative sentences like "Stray Kids produce their own songs" and "Hwasa is very sexy." Let's break it down:

- 스트레이 키즈는 노래를 직접 작곡해요. (Seuteurei Kijeu-neun norae-reul jikjeop jakgokhaeyo) - *Stray Kids-particle their song-particle directly compose.*
- 화사는 진짜 섹시해요. (Hwasa-neun jinjja seksihada) - *Hwasa-particle very sexy is.*

Now, in this chapter, you will learn how to form negative sentences, like "I don't sing" or "She is not a rapper" and inquisitive sentences, like "Do you dance?" or "Is he a producer?" We will also go beyond the yes/no questions and learn to ask what, who, when, where, which, and how. 준비됐어? (junbi dwaesseo) - Are you ready?

NEGATIVE SENTENCES

Negation in Korean sentences can be expressed in several ways. The two most common methods are using 안 **(an)** and -지 않다 **(-ji anta)**. Each method has its nuances and preferred contexts. Here's an explanation of how each works:

Using 안 (an)

The particle 안 **(an)** is placed *before* the conjugated verb or adjective to negate it. This method is straightforward and commonly used in everyday conversation.

Structure: 안 + Verb/Adjective

Examples:

1. Present Tense:

 -하다 **(hada) - to do** → 안 해요 **(an haeyo)** - I don't do

 -먹다 **(meokda) - to eat** → 안 먹어요 **(an meogeoyo)** - I don't eat

 -가다 **(gada) - to go** → 안 가요 **(an gayo)** - I don't go

2. Past Tense:

 -하다 **(hada) - to do** → 안 했어요 **(an haesseoyo)** - I didn't do

 -먹다 **(meokda) - to eat** → 안 먹었어요 **(an meogeosseoyo)** - I didn't eat

 -가다 **(gada) - to go** → 안 갔어요 **(an gasseoyo)** - I didn't go

Using -지 않다 (-ji anta)

Attach -지 않다 **(-ji anta)** to the verb stem to negate it. 않다 **(anta)** is a verb in Korean that means "not" or "do not," and is used to negate other verbs and adjectives, indicating that an action or state does not occur or exist. This form is slightly more formal and can be used in both written and spoken Korean.

You must conjugate 않다 by following the regular conjugation rules.

Structure: Verb Stem + -지 않다 (-ji anta)

Examples:

1. Present Tense:

 -하다 **(hada) - to do** → 하지 않아요 **(haji anayo)** - I don't do

 -먹다 **(meokda) - to eat** → 먹지 않아요 **(meokji anayo)** - I don't eat

 -가다 **(gada) - to go** → 가지 않아요 **(gaji anayo)** - I don't go

2. Past Tense:

 -하다 **(hada) - to do** → 하지 않았어요 **(haji anasseoyo)** - I didn't do

-먹다 (meokda) - to eat → 먹지 않았어요 (meokji anasseoyo) - I didn't eat

-가다 (gada) - to go → 가지 않았어요 (gaji anasseoyo) - I didn't go

Here is the conjugation rule summary table for 않다:

Tense	Informal	Polite	Polite with -시 (si)	Formal
Present	않아 (ana)	않아요 (anayo)	않으세요 (aneuseyo)	않습니다 (anseumnida)
Past	않았어 (anasseo)	않았어요 (anasseoyo)	않으셨어요 (aneusyeosseoyo)	않았습니다 (anasseumnida)
Future	않을 거야 (aneul geoya)	않을 거예요 (aneul geoyeyo)	않으실 거예요 (aneusil geoyeyo)	않을 것입니다 (aneul geosimnida)

안 vs. -지 않다 Comparison

The difference boils down to the following:

- **안 (an):** Simple and commonly used in daily conversation. It is less formal and straightforward.
- **-지 않다 (-ji anta):** More formal and can be used in both spoken and written contexts.

Negative Imperative - "Do not"

When prohibiting someone from doing something, use **-지 마 (ji ma)** in informal settings or **-지 마세요 (ji maseyo)** for polite settings.

Structure: Verb stem + **-지 마 (ji ma)** or **- 지 마세요 (ji maseyo)**

Examples (polite):

-하다 (hada) - to do → 하지 마세요 (haji maseyo) - (Please) don't do.

-먹다 (meokda) - to eat → 먹지 마세요 (meokji maseyo) - (Please) don't eat.

-가다 (gada) - to go → 가지 마세요 (gaji maseyo) - (Please) don't go.

Negative Propositive - "Let's not"

When advising or persuading someone against doing something, use -지 말자 (ji malja). Note that this suffix is used only for informal settings among peers or friends. (For polite or formal settings, you would phrase it more indirectly to soften the tone.)

Structure: Verb stem + -지 말자 **(ji malja)**

Examples (informal):

-하다 **(hada) - to do** → 하지 말자 **(haji malja)** - Let's not do it.

-먹다 **(meokda) - to eat** → 먹지 말자 **(meokji malja)** - Let's not eat.

-가다 **(gada) - to go** → 가지 말자 **(gaji malja)** - Let's not go.

NEGATION OF MODAL VERBS

Negating modal verbs in Korean involves using the negative form of the modal verb construction. Here are the key modal verbs "cannot," "may not," "must not," and their respective structures and examples.

1. -ㄹ/을 수 없다 (-l/eul su eopda) - Cannot

To express inability or impossibility, use the structure -ㄹ / 을 수 없다.

Structure:

- Verb stem + -을 수 없다 (-eul su eopda) — if the verb stem ends in a consonant
- Verb stem + -ㄹ 수 없다 (-l su eopda) — if the verb stem ends in a vowel
- For all 하다 verbs, replace 하다 with 할 수 없다 (-hal su eopda)

없다 **(eopda)** is a regular verb that follows the following rules:

Tense	Informal	Polite	Polite with 시 (si)	Formal
Present	없어 (eopseo)	없어요 (eopseoyo)	없으세요 (eopseuseyo)	없습니다 (eopseumnida)
Past	없었어 (eopseosseo)	없었어요 (eopseosseoyo)	없으셨어요 (eopseusyeosseoyo)	없었습니다 (eopseotseumnida)
Future	없을 거야 (eopseul geoya)	없을 거예요 (eopseul geoyeyo)	없으실 거예요 (eopseusil geoyeyo)	없을 것입니다 (eopseul geosimnida)

Examples (polite form):

- 새 앨범을 구할 **수 없어요**. (Sae aelbeomeul guha**l su eopseoyo**.) — I can't find / get the new album.
- 내일 만날 **수 없어요**. (Naeil manna-**l su eopseoyo**.) — I can't meet tomorrow.

An easier alternative: 못 (mot) also means "cannot."

You just have to put it before the verb, just like in English. For example, 못 먹어요 (mot meogeoyo) means "cannot eat" or "unable to eat."

However, 못 is slightly different from -ㄹ/을 수 없다 when describing skills and capacities. In this context, 못 implies "not well." For example, 노래 못 해요 (norae mot haeyo) means "cannot sing (well)" – and not that they are physically incapable of singing.

2. 하면 안 되다 (ha-myeon an doeda) - May Not/Must Not

To express prohibition, as in, "may not" or "must not," use the structure -으면 안 되다 (eumyeon an doeda) or -면 안 되다 (myeon an doeda). 면 (myeon), a particle meaning "if," in combination with 안 되다, expresses prohibition.

Structure:

- **Verb stem + -으면 안 되다 (-eumyeon an doeda)** — if the verb stem ends in a consonant
- **Verb stem + -면 안 되다 (-myeon an doeda)** — if the verb stem ends in a vowel, including 하다 verbs.

Examples:

- 여기서 뭐 먹**으면 안 돼요**. (Yeogiseo mwo meog**eumyeon an dwaeyo**.) — You may not eat here.
- 지금 가**면 안 돼요**. (Jigeum ga**myeon an dwaeyo**.) — You may not go now.
- 여기서 연습하**면 안 돼요**. (Yeogiseo yeonseup-ha**myeon an dwaeyo**.) — You may not practice here.
- 거짓말하**면 안 돼요**. (Geojinmal-ha**myeon an dwaeyo**.) — You must not lie.

INQUISITIVE FORMS

In Korean, inquisitive forms (questions) are created in different ways depending on whether you are asking a yes/no question or using question words like "what," "who," "when," "where," and "how." For both types of questions, remember that the subject of the sentence is often omitted. This is especially true with "you" when posing a question directly to someone about them; "you" is almost always omitted.

Here's a breakdown:

예/아니요 질문 (ye/aniyo jilmun) - Yes/No Questions

Forming yes/no questions in Korean is pretty straightforward. Just follow these steps:

Using Question Marks and Questioning Intonation

Yes/no questions can be formed by using the same word order as statements but adding a question mark when writing or a questioning intonation when speaking. This method is mostly used in informal and polite forms.

Example (polite form):

- **Statement**: 그는 래퍼예요. (Geuneun raeppeo-yeyo.) - He is a rapper.
- **Question**: 그는 래퍼예요? (Geuneun raeppeo-yeyo?) - Is he a rapper?

Using Interrogative Particles

You can also form questions by adding various endings to the sentence which vary according to context, speaker-listener relationship, and politeness level. Here are the most important ones to know:

Informal Question Endings: These endings are used among close friends, peers, or in casual situations. They convey a sense of familiarity and directness.

1. -니 (ni)

Usage: Commonly used by older adults when speaking to someone younger (e.g. mom to her son).

Connotation: Soft, friendly, and slightly literary (you would see this ending often in a children's storybook.)

Examples:

- 어디 가니? (Eodi ga**ni**?) - Where are you going?
- 뭐 하니? (Mwo ha**ni**?) - What are you doing?

2. -냐 (nya)

Usage: More commonly used among close friends

Connotation: Slangy, casual, direct, slightly rough

Examples:

- 어디 가냐? (Eodi ga**nya**?) - Where are you going?
- 뭐 하냐? (Mwo ha**nya**?) - What are you doing?

3. -까 (-kka)

Usage: Used to propose an activity or ask for opinions among friends.

Connotation: Friendly and casual

Examples:

- 같이 갈까? (Gachi gal**kka**?) - Shall we go together?
- 뭐 할까? (Mwo hal**kka**?) - What shall we do?

4. -지 (-ji)

Usage: Used to ask questions in an open-ended manner. This often sounds like the speaker is thinking out loud or talking to themself. When said to another person, this ending invites suggestions but does not expect answers.

Examples:

- 어디 가지? (Eodi ga**ji**?) - Where should I/we go?
- 뭐 하지? (Mwo ha**ji**?) - What am I/are we going to do?

Polite Question Endings: These endings are used in everyday conversation to show politeness without being overly formal. They are suitable for most social interactions.

1. -세요 (-seyo)

Usage: Used to show curiosity or politeness without being too formal.

Connotation: Gentle and inquisitive.

Examples:

- 어디 가**세요**? (Eodi ga**seyo**?) - Where are you going?
- 뭐 하**세요**? (Mwo ha**seyo**?) - What are you doing?

2. -까요 (-kkayo)

Usage: Used for offering, suggesting, or confirming politely.

Connotation: Polite and tentative.

Examples:

- 같이 갈**까요**? (Gachi gal**kkayo**?) - Shall we go together?
- 이거 할**까요**? (Igeo hal**kkayo**?) - Shall we do this?

__Formal Question Endings:__ This ending is used in some public speeches or strictly hierarchical environments. It sounds too rigid and is rarely used in everyday conversations.

-ㅂ니까(-mnikka) / 습니까 (-seumnikka) / 십니까 (-simnikka)

Usage: Often used in settings such as the national assembly, court-rooms, and the military.

Connotation: Extremely formal and respectful

Examples:

- 어디 가**십니까**? (Eodi ga**simnikka**?) - Where are you going, sir/madam?
- 무엇을 하**십니까**? (Mueoseul ha**simnikka**?) - What are you doing, sir/madam?

Yes and No in the Korean Language

Now, let's look into how to answer yes/no questions in Korean, as it is a bit different from European languages.

In Korean, there are several ways to say "yes" and "no," depending on the context and the level of formality. Here are the most common expressions:

Yes:

1. 예 (ye)/네 (ne): These are the most common polite ways to say "yes" in Korean. 네 can be used in almost any situation, including when you want to say "you're welcome." This is your go-to.

2. 응 (eung): This is a casual way to say "yes" to your friends and family, similar to "yep" or "uh-huh" in English. When 응 is pronounced more bluntly, it becomes 어 (eo), which is even more casual and typically used among very close friends.

3. 맞아요 (majayo): This means "that's right" or "that's correct" and is used to agree with someone or confirm a statement.

No:

1. 아니요 (aniyo): This is the most common and polite way to say "no" in Korean.

2. 아니 (ani): This is a casual way to say "no" and often used in informal conversations with friends or family.

3. 안 돼요 (an dwaeyo): This means "it can't be done" or "it's not possible" and is used to express impossibility or prohibition.

4. 아니에요 (ani-eyo): This means "that's not it" or "that's not the case" and is used to disagree with someone or correct a statement.

If you are not sure which one to use, the rule of thumb is to use polite expressions like 네 and 아니요 when speaking to someone you do not know very well.

Note on answering Korean yes/no questions: You might think that answering yes/no questions is a no-brainer: a yes is a yes, and a no is a no, right? But not so fast! In Korean — as in other Asian languages — the answer depends on how the question is phrased. Let's take a look at the examples:

Example 1: Let's say you know that Lisa is Thai. If someone asks...

Q: 리사는 태국 사람이에요? (Lisa-neun taeguk saram-ieyo?) — Lisa is Thai? You would answer...

A: 네, 리사는 태국 사람이에요. (Ne, Lisa-neun taeguk saram-ieyo) — Yes, Lisa is Thai.

On the other hand, if someone asks...

Q: 리사는 태국 사람 아니죠*? (Lisa-neun taeguk saram anijyo?) — Lisa isn't Thai? Then you would answer…

A: 아니요, 리사는 태국 사람이에요. (Aniyo, Lisa-neun taeguk saram-ieyo) — **No**, Lisa *is* Thai.

Example 2: You know that Hyunjin is *not* the Main Dancer of his group. So if someone asks…

Q: 현진은 메인 댄서예요? (Hyeonjin-eun mein daenseo-yeyo?) — Hyunjin is the Main Dancer? You would answer…

A: 아니요, 현진은 메인 댄서 아니에요. (Aniyo, Hyeonjin-eun mein daenseo anieyo.) — No, Hyunjin is not the Main Dancer.

On the other hand, if someone asks…

Q: 현진은 메인 댄서 아니죠*? (Hyeonjin-eun mein daenseo anijyo?) — Hyunjin isn't the Main Dancer?

A: 네, 현진은 메인 댄서 아니에요. (Ne, Hyeonjin-eun mein daenseo anieyo.) — **Yes**, Hyunjin is *not* the Main Dancer.

*죠 (jyo) is added to the end of a statement to seek confirmation. It is comparable to "right?" or "isn't it?" in English.

In both cases, you are affirming or negating the underlying assumption behind the question. Hope we haven't lost you.

Open Questions Using Question Words

When forming "open" questions, i.e., non-yes/no questions, much like in English, you use specific question words like "what" and "how." The sentence structure typically follows the Subject-Object-Verb (SOV) order, with the question word placed at the beginning of the sentence or before the verb.

Common Question Words:

1. 뭐 **(mwo)** / 무엇 **(mueot)** — What
2. 누구 **(nugu)** — Who
3. 언제 **(eonje)** — When
4. 어디 **(eodi)** — Where
5. 왜 **(wae)** — Why
6. 어느 **(eoneu)** — Which
7. 어떻게 **(eotteoke)** — How

Let's go over them one by one.

1. 무엇 (muot)/뭐 (mwo) - What:

뭐 is a shortened version of 무엇 and is more frequently used; 무엇 is almost never used.

 -**What is this?** - Use the verb 이다 (ida), "to be."

Informal: 이게 **뭐**야? (Ige **mwo**ya?)

- 이게 — This thing
- 뭐 — What
- 야? — is?

Polite: 이게 **뭐**예요? (Ige **mwo**yeyo?)

- 이게 — This thing
- 뭐 — What
- 예요? — is?

 -**What is your name?** — Use the verb 이다 (ida), "to be."

Informal: 이름이 **뭐**야? (Ireumi **mwo**ya?)

- 이름 — Name
- 이 — subject particle
- 뭐 — what
- 야? — is?

Polite: 이름이 **뭐**예요? (Ireumi **mwo**yeyo?)

- 이름 — Name
- 이 — subject particle
- 뭐 — what
- 예요 — is?

 -**What changed?** — Here, "what" is the subject of the sentence, followed by an action verb.

Informal: **뭐**가 바뀌었어? (**Mwo**ga bakkwieosseo?)

- 뭐 — What
- 가 — Subject particle

- 바뀌었어? — Changed?

Polite: 뭐가 바뀌었어요? (**Mwo**ga bakkwieosseoyo?)

- 뭐 — What
- 가 — Subject particle
- 바뀌었어요? — changed?

-**What do you eat?/What are you eating?** — "What" is the object of the sentence. Note that you can simply use the present tense instead of progressive, as it is usually clear from context that you want to know what they are eating *now*.

Informal: 뭐 먹어? (**Mwo** meogeo?)

- 뭐 — What
- 먹어?— (you) eat?

Polite: 뭐 먹어요? (**Mwo** meogeoyo?)

- 뭐 — What
- 먹어요? — (you) eat?

Note that, in casual speech, 뭐 (mwo) is used without the object particle.

2. 누가 (nuga), 누구 (nugu) - Who: Use 누가 when "who" is the subject of the sentence, and 누구 when it is the object of the sentence (like "whom" in English).

-**Who are you?** — Use the verb 이다 (ida), "to be."

Informal: 누구야? (**Nugu**ya?)

- 누구 — Who
- 야? — is (it)?

Polite: 누구예요? (**Nugu**yeyo?)

- 누구 — Who
- 예요?— is (it)?

Also polite: 누구세요*? (**Nugu**seyo?)

- 누구 — Who

- 세요?— are (you)?

The honorific 시, which is conjugated into 세, shows respect to the listener. Therefore, even when the subject of the sentence ("you") is omitted, the listener understands that the speech is directed at them.

Formal: 누구십니까? (**Nugu**simnikka?)

- 누구 — Who
- 십니까?— are (you)?

-**Who is your bias?** — Use the verb 이다 (ida), "to be."

*Informal:*최애가 **누구**야? (Choe-ae-ga **nugu**ya?)

- 최애 — bias
- 가 — subject particle
- 누구 — who
- 야? — is?

Polite: 최애가 **누구**예요? (Choe-ae-ga **nugu**yeyo?)

- 최애 — bias
- 가 — subject particle
- 누구 — who
- 예요? — is?

-**Who came?** — "Who" is the subject of the sentence.

Informal: **누가** 왔어? (**Nuga** wasseo?)

- 누가 — Who (as the subject of sentence)
- 왔어? — came?

Polite: **누가** 왔어요? (**Nuga** wasseoyo?)

- 누가 — Who (as the subject of sentence)
- 왔어요? — came?

-**Who do you like?** — "Who" is the object of the sentence.

Informal: **누구** 좋아해? (**Nugu** joahae?)

- 누구 — Who
- 좋아해? — (you) like?

Polite: 누구 좋아해요? (**Nugu** joahaeyo?)

- 누구 — Who
- 좋아해요? — (you) like?

3. 언제 (eonje) - When:

-**When is your birthday?** — Use the verb 이다 (ida), "to be."

Informal: 생일이 **언제**야? (Saengil-i **eonje**ya?)

- 생일 — (Your) birthday
- 이 — subjective particle
- 언제 — when
- 야? — is?

Polite: 생일이 **언제**예요? (Saengil-i **eonje**yeyo?)

- 생일 — (Your) birthday
- 이 — subjective particle
- 언제 — when
- 예요? — is?

-**When did they debut?**

Informal: **언제** 데뷔했어? (**Eonje** debwihaesseo?)

- 언제 — when
- 데뷔했어? — (they) debuted?

Polite: **언제** 데뷔했어요? (**Eonje** debwihaesseoyo?)

- 언제 — when
- 데뷔했어요? — (they) debuted?

Formal: **언제** 데뷔했습니까? (**Eonje** debwihaesseumnikka?)

- 언제 — when
- 데뷔했습니까? — (they) debuted?

-When will they come to America?

Informal: **언제** 미국에 올까? (**Eonje** miguge olkka?)

- 언제 — when
- 미국 — America
- 에 — location particle
- 올까? — will (they) come?

Polite: **언제** 미국에 올까요? (**Eonje** miguge olkkayo?)

- 언제 — when
- 미국 — America
- 에 — location particle
- 올까요? — will (they) come?

4. 어디 (eodi) - Where:

-Where is the concert? — Use the verb 이다 (ida), "to be."

Informal: 콘서트가 **어디**야? (Konseoteuga **eodi**ya?)

- 콘서트 — Concert
- 가 — subject particle
- 어디 — where
- 야? — is?

Polite: 콘서트가 **어디**예요? (Konseoteuga **eodi** yeyo?)

- 콘서트 — Concert
- 가 — subject particle
- 어디 — where
- 예요? — is?

-Where are you from?

Informal: **어디**서 왔어? (**Eodi**seo wasseo?)

- 어디 — where
- 서 — connector for "from"
- 왔어? — (you) came?

Polite: **어디**서 왔어요? (**Eodiseo** wasseoyo?)

- 어디 — where
- 서 — connector for "from"
- 왔어요? — (you) came?

Also polite: **어디**서 오셨어요*? (**Eodi**seo osyeosseoyo?)

- 어디 — where
- 서 — connector for "from"
- 오셨어요? — (you) came?

* The honorific 시, conjugated as 셨 in the past tense, shows respect to the listener. In short, both 왔어요 and 오셨어요 are correct in this context, but the latter is slightly more proper.

Formal: **어디**서 오셨습니까? (**Eodi**seo osyeosseumnikka?)

- 어디 — where
- 서 — connector for "from"
- 오셨습니까? — (you) came?

-**Where does she/he live?**

Informal: 걔 **어디** 살아? (Gye **eodi** sara?)

- 걔 — that person (gender-neutral; casual)
- 어디 — where
- 살아? — live

Polite: 걔 **어디** 살아요? (Gye **eodi** sarayo?)

- 걔 — that person
- 어디 — where
- 살아요?— live?

5. 왜 (wae) - Why:

-Why are they going to Paris?

Informal: 파리에 **왜** 가? (Pari-e **wae** ga?)

- 파리 — Paris
- 에 — location particle
- 왜— why

- 가? — (they) go?

Polite: 파리에 **왜** 가요? (Pari-e **wae** gayo?)

- 파리 — Paris
- 에 — location particle
- 왜— why
- 가요? — (they) go?

-Why did he leave the team?

Informal: **왜** 팀에서 탈퇴했어? (**Wae** timeseo taltoehaesseo?)

- 왜— why
- 팀 — team
- 에서 — from
- 탈퇴했어? — (he) left?

Polite: **왜** 팀에서 탈퇴했어요? (**Wae** timeseo taltoehaesseoyo?)

- 왜— why
- 팀 — team
- 에서 — from
- 탈퇴했어요? — (he) left?

Formal: **왜** 팀에서 탈퇴했습니까? (**Wae** timeseo taltoehaesseumnikka?)

- 왜— why
- 팀 — team
- 에서 — from
- 탈퇴했습니까? — (he) left?

6. 어느 (eoneu) - Which:

-Which member is the Visual? — Use the verb "이다."

Informal: **어느** 멤버가 비주얼이야? (**Eoneu** membeoga bijueoriya?)

- 어느 — Which
- 멤버 — member
- 가 — subject particle
- 비주얼 — visual
- 이야? — is?

Polite: **어느** 멤버가 비주얼이에요? (**Eoneu** membeoga bijueorieyo?)

- 어느 — Which
- 멤버 — member
- 가 — subject particle
- 비주얼 — visual
- 이에요? — is?

Formal: **어느** 멤버가 비주얼입니까? (**Eoneu** membeoga bijue-orimnikka?)

- 어느 — Which
- 멤버 — member
- 가 — subject particle
- 비주얼 — visual
- 입니까? — is?

-Which group do you support?

Informal: **어느** 그룹 응원해? (**Eoneu** geurup eungwonhae?)

- 어느 — Which
- 그룹 — group
- 응원해? — (you) support?

Polite: **어느** 그룹 응원해요? (**Eoneu** geurup eungwonhaeyo?)

- 어느 — Which
- 그룹 — group
- 응원해요? — (you) support?

Also polite: **어느** 그룹 응원하세요*? (**Eoneu** geurup eungwonhaseyo?)

- 어느 — Which
- 그룹 — group
- 응원하세요? — (you) support?

* The honorific 시, conjugated as 세 in the present tense, shows respect to the listener.

7. 어떻게 (eotteoke), 어때 (eottae), 어때요 (eottaeyo), 어떻습니까 (eotteosseumnikka) - How:

어떻게 (eotteoke) — Use this to ask about the manner or method of doing something.

  -How do you do it?

Informal: 어떻게 해? (**Eotteoke** hae?)

Polite: 어떻게 해요? (**Eotteoke** haeyo?)

Formal: 어떻게 합니까? (**Eotteoke** hamnikka?)

어때 (eottae), 어때요 (eottaeyo), 어떻습니까 (eotteosseumnikka) — Used to ask about the condition or quality of something.

  -How is the food at this place/restaurant?

Informal: 이 집 음식 **어때**? (I jip eumsik **eottae**?)

- 이 — This
- 집 — place (While 집 literally means "house," it is very commonly used to mean "restaurant" in this context.)
- 음식 — food
- 어때? — how is?

Polite: 이 집 음식 **어때요**? (I jip eumsik **eottaeyo**?)

- 이 식당 음식 — This restaurant food
- 어때요? — how is?

Formal: 이 식당 음식 **어떻습니까**? (I sikdang eumsik **eotteosseumnikka**?)

- 이 식당 음식 — This restaurant food
- 어떻습니까? — how is?

8. Other "How"s:

몇 (myeot)

몇 is used to ask about quantity, usually translated as "how many."

Examples:

- 몇 명이에요? (**Myeot** myeong-ieyo?) - How many are they?

- 몇 곡 불렀어요? (**Myeot** gok bulleosseoyo?) — How many songs did they perform?
- 몇 시에요? (**Myeot** si-eyo?) - What time is it?

얼마나 (*eolmana*)

얼마나 is used to ask about the extent, degree, or amount, often translated as "how much" or "how many."

- **얼마나** 커요? (**Eolmana** keoyo?) - How big is it?
- **얼마나** 걸려요? (**Eolmana** geollyeoyo?) - How long does it take?
- 관객 소리가 **얼마나** 컸어요? (Gwangaek soriga **eolmana** keosseoyo?) - How loud was the audience?

얼마 (*eolma*)

얼마 is used to ask about price or cost, usually translated as "how much."

- 이거 **얼마**예요? (Igeo **eolma**-yeyo?) - How much is this?
- 티켓 **얼마**였어요? (Tiket **eolma**-yeosseoyo?) - How much was the ticket?

Well, now that you know the basics, you are ready to put them to practice. First step? Some real life phrases!

EIGHT
EVERYDAY PHRASES
FOR EVERYDAY SITUATIONS

AS YOU CAN PROBABLY IMAGINE, it is impossible to list ALL the phrases you will need for every possible situation you may encounter — even as a tourist — in Korea.

But here is our attempt at it, just to get you started on the right path:

인사 (INSA) - GREETINGS

1. 안녕하세요 (**an-nyeong-ha-se-yo**) - Hello (polite)

2. 잘 가 (**jal ga**) - Goodbye : *Well-go* (informal)

3. 안녕 (**an-nyeong**) - Hi/Bye (informal)

4. 안녕히 가세요 (**annyeonghi gaseyo**) - Goodbye; when the other person is leaving (polite)

5. 안녕히 계세요 (**annyeonghi gyeseyo**) - Goodbye; when you are leaving and the other person is staying (polite)

6. 다녀오겠습니다 (**da-nyeo o-get-seum-ni-da**) - I'm leaving now: *will-go-and-come-back*; This is a polite way of saying goodbye to someone who sees you out, usually your parents. The casual version 갔다올게 (**gatdaolge**) is more commonly used because most families use informal speech to express intimacy.

7. 다녀오세요 (**da-nyeo-o-se-yo**) - Have a good trip: *go-and-come-back*;

This is a polite way of saying goodbye to someone leaving home, usually your parents.

8. 다녀왔습니다 (da-nyeo wass-seum-ni-da) - I'm back: *came-back*; This is a phrase you say when you come home.

9. 잘 다녀 왔어요? (jal da-nyeo-wass-eo-yo) - Welcome home: *Well went-and-came-back*; You can simply say 왔어? (wass-eo), which means "you came?," when your family member comes home.

10. 어서 오세요 (eo-seo o-se-yo) - Welcome (to a store or establishment): *Come-quickly*; You would hear this sometimes when you walk into a restaurant.

11. 환영합니다 (hwan-yeong-ham-ni-da) - Welcome

12. 잘 먹겠습니다 (jal meok-get-seum-ni-da) - I will eat well: This is a phrase you say before you start eating, similar to "bon appetit." The expression implies gratitude for the person who prepared the meal.

13. 잘 먹었습니다 (jal meo-geo-sseum-ni-da) - I ate well: This is a phrase you say at the end of a meal.

14. 좋은 아침(이에요) (joe-un a-chim-i-e-yo) - Good morning

15. 잘 자요 (jal-ja-yo) - Good night: *Well sleep*

16. 건강하세요 (geon-gang-ha-se-yo) - Stay healthy

17. 조심히 가세요 (jo-sim-hi ga-se-yo) - Go safely

18. 축하합니다 (chuk-ha-ham-ni-da) - Congratulations

19. 생일 축하해요 (saeng-il chuk-ha-hae-yo) - Happy birthday

20. 메리 크리스마스 (me-ri keu-ri-seu-ma-seu) - Merry Christmas

21. 새해 복 많이 받으세요 (sae-hae bok mani ba-deu-se-yo) - Happy New Year: *New year-blessings-many-receive*

소개 (SOGAE) - INTRODUCTION

22. 만나서 반가워요 (man-na-seo ban-ga-wo-yo) - Nice to meet you

23. 제 이름은 [Name]이에요/예요 (je ireum-eun [Name] i-e-yo/ye-yo) - My name is [Name]

24. 이름이 뭐예요? (I-reum-i mwo-ye-yo?) - What is your name?: *Name what-is?*

25. 저는 [Country]에서 왔어요 (jeo-neun [Country] eseo wa-sseo-yo) - I'm from [Country]

26. 어디서 왔어요? (eo-di-seo wa-sseo-yo?) - Where are you from?: *Where-from-came?*

27. 저는 [미국인]이에요 (jeo-neun [mi-gu-gin] i-e-yo) - I am [American]

28. 한국인이에요? (han-gu-gin-i-e-yo?) - Are you Korean?

29. 저는 [Age]살이에요 (jeo-neun [Age] sa-ri-e-yo) - I am [Age] years old

30. 몇 살이에요? (myeot sa-ri-e-yo?) - How old are you?

31. 저는 [Profession]이에요/예요 (jeoneun [Profession] i-e-yo/ye-yo) - I am a [Profession]

32. 무슨 일 하세요? (mu-seun il ha-se-yo?) - What do you do?: *What-work-do?*

33. 저는 [place name or address]에 살아요 (jeo-neun [place name or address] ae sa-ra-yo) - I live in/at [place name or address]

34. 어디 살아요? (Eo-di sa-ra-yo?) - Where do you live?

35. 영어 할 수 있어요? (yeong-eo hal su i-sseo-yo?) - Can you speak English?

36. 한국어 할 수 있어요? (han-gu-geo hal su i-sseo-yo?) - Can you speak Korean?

37. 저는 한국어를 조금 해요 (jeoneun hangugeoreul jogeum haeyo) - I speak a little Korean

감사와 사과 (GAMSAWA SAGWA) - GRATITUDE & APOLOGY

38. 감사합니다 (gam-sa-ham-ni-da) - Thank you (formal)

39. 고마워요 (go-ma-wo-yo) - Thank you (polite)

40. 고마워 (go ma-wo) - Thank you (informal)

41. 정말 감사해요 (jeong-mal gam-sa-hae-yo) - Thank you very much

42. 아니에요 (anieyo) - It's nothing: meaning "You are welcome"

(Alternatively, you can simply answer with 네 (ne), much like saying "sure" or "of course" in English when someone thanks you.)

43. 미안합니다 (**mi-an-ham-ni-da**) - I'm sorry (formal)

44. 미안해요 (**mi-an-hae-yo**) - I'm sorry (polite)

45. 미안해 (**mi-an-hae**) - I'm sorry (informal)

46. 실례합니다 (**sil-lye-ham-ni-da**) - Excuse me (for interrupting)

47. 와주서서 감사합니다 (**wa-ju-syeo-seo gam-sa-ham-ni-da**) - Thank you for coming

질문 (JILMUN) - QUESTIONS

48. 이게 뭐예요? (**i-ge mwo-ye-yo**) - What is this?

49. 뭐 해요? (**mwo hae-yo**) - What are you doing?

50. 몇 시예요? (**myeot si-ye-yo**) - What time is it?

51. 무슨 일이에요? (**mu-seun ir-i-e-yo**) - What's the matter?

52. 무슨 뜻이에요? (**mu-seun tteu-si-e-yo**) - What does it mean?: *What-meaning-is?*

53. 무슨 색이에요? (**mu-seun sae-gi-e-yo**) - What color is it?: *What-color-is?*

54. 전화번호 뭐예요? (**jeon-hwa-beon-ho mwo-ye-yo**) - What's your (phone) number?: *(Phone) number what-is?*

55. 잘 지냈어요? (**jal ji-nae-sseo-yo**) - How have you been?

56. 얼마예요? (**eol-ma-ye-yo**) - How much is it?

57. 이거 얼마예요? (**i-geo eol-ma-ye-yo**) - How much is this?

58. 날씨가 어때요? (**nal-ssi-ga eo-ttae-yo**) - How's the weather?: *Weather how-is?*

59. 언제예요? (**eon-je-ye-yo**) - When is it?: *When is?*

60. 언제 와요? (**eon-je wa-yo**) - When are you coming?: *When come?*

61. 화장실 어디에요? (**hwa-jang-sil eo-di-e-yo**) - Where is the bathroom?: *Bathroom where-is?*

62. 어디 가요? (**eo-di ga-yo**) - Where are you going?: *Where go?*

63. 왜 그래요? (**wae geu-rae-yo**) - What's the matter?/What's going on?: *Why (is it) like that?*

이해 (IHAE) - UNDERSTANDING

64. 그러네요 **(geu-reo-ne-yo)** - I see

65. 당연하죠! **(dang-yeon-ha-jyo)** - Of course!

66. 이해했어요 **(i-hae-hae-sseo-yo)** - I understand

67. 이해 못했어요 **(i-hae mo-taesseo-yo)** - I don't understand

68. 알겠어요 **(al-ge-sseo-yo)** - Got it; okay

69. 모르겠어요 **(mo-reu-ge-sseo-yo)** - I don't know / I'm not sure

감정, 상태, 그리고 의견 (GAMJEONG, SANGTAE, GEURIGO UIGYEON) - FEELING, STATE, AND OPINION

70. 슬퍼요 **(seul-peo-yo)** - I'm sad

71. 기뻐요 **(gi-bbeo-yo)** - I'm happy

72. 배고파요 **(bae-go-pa-yo)** - I'm hungry

73. 목말라요 **(mong-mal-la-yo)** - I'm thirsty

74. 배불러요 **(bae-bul-leo-yo)** - I'm full

75. 졸려요 **(jol-lyeo-yo)** - I'm sleepy

76. 피곤해요 **(pi-gon-hae-yo)** - I'm tired

77. 아파요 **(a-pa-yo)** - It hurts

78. 걱정 마세요 **(geok-jeong ma-se-yo)** - Don't worry

79. 기분이 어때요? **(gi-bun-i eo-ttae-yo?)** - How do you feel?

80. 좋아요* **(jo-a-yo)** - Sure, okay (approval) / it's good

81. 좋아해요* **(joahaeyo)** - (I) like someone / something

Note: What's the difference between 좋아요 (joayo) and 좋아해요 (joahaeyo)? — is a question we get a lot, because these two phrases often seem to be used interchangeably. Let's clarify:

좋아요 **(joayo):** The subject is a thing or an idea that appeals to you in that moment; you use this expression to describe something as good, ideal, delicious, etc.

Examples:

- Q. 새 노래 어때요 (sae norae eottaeyo)? How is the new song?
- A. 좋아요 (joayo)! It's good!

- Q. 세시에 만날까요 (sesie mannalkkayo)? Should we meet at 3?
- A. 좋아요 (joayo)! Sure!

좋아해요 (joahaeyo): The subject is "I"; you use this expression to talk about your strong preferences (that are not likely to change) or when you have a crush on someone.

Examples:

- 커피 좋아해요 (keopi joahaeyo). I like coffee.
- 베이비몬스터 좋아해요 (beibimonseuteo joahaeyo). I like BABYMONSTER.
- 자전거 타는 거 좋아해요 (jajeongeo taneun geo joahaeyo). I like riding bikes.

82. 싫어요 (sireo-yo) - No (refusal); I don't like it

83. 재미있어요 (jae-mi i-sseo-yo) - It's fun

84. 맛있어요 (masi-sseo-yo) - It's delicious

85. 맛없어요 (mat-eop-seo-yo) - It's not tasty

86. 괜찮아요 (gwaen-chan-a-yo) - It's okay; no worries

87. 차가워요 (cha-ga-wo-yo) - It's cold – to the touch; when something is cold

88. 뜨거워요 (tteu-geo-wo-yo) - It's hot - to the touch; when something is hot

89. 추워요 (chu-wo-yo) - It's cold - weather-wise

90. 더워요 (deo-wo-yo) - It's hot - weather-wise

91. 비가 와요 (bi-ga wa-yo) - It's raining: *Rain comes*

92. 눈이 와요 (nuni wa-yo) - It's snowing: *Snow comes*

93. 바람이 불어요 (ba-rami-bu-reo-yo) - It's windy: *Wind blows*

94. 날씨가 좋아요 (nal-ssi-ga jo-a-yo) - The weather is nice

요청 (YOCHEONG) & 명령 (MYEONGNYEONG) - REQUESTS & COMMANDS

In Korean, forming request phrases is straightforward and involves polite endings. Here's a guide on how to form two types of request phrases: **"Please do [something]"** and **"Please don't do [something]"**.

Please do [something]

To make a polite request asking someone to do something, use the verb stem + -아/어/여 주세요 (depending on the vowel in the verb stem). Although 주세요 is derived from the verb 주다, meaning "to give," it does not carry that meaning as an auxiliary verb in a request sentence. Instead, it functions like the English word "please."

Structure:

- Stem + 아 주세요 **(a juseyo)** if the stem ends in ㅏ or ㅗ.
- Stem + 어 주세요 **(eo juseyo)** if the stem ends in any other vowel.
- Setem + 여 주세요 **(yeo juseyo)** if the stem ends in 하 → -해 주세요 **(hae juseyo)** due to contraction.

Please don't do [something]

To politely request someone not to do something, use the verb stem + -지 마세요 **(ji maseyo)**.

Examples of both forms can be found in the following list of requests and commands:

95. 저기요 **(jeo-gi-yo)** - Excuse me: *Over there* (implying you are calling out to someone who is at some distance.)

96. [뭐] 주세요 **([mwo] juseyo)** - Please give me [something]: *[Something] please*

97. 계산서 주세요 **(gye-san-seo ju-se-yo)** - Check, please

98. 물 좀 주세요 **(mul jom ju-se-yo)** - Please give me some water: *Water some please*

99. 더 주세요 **(deo ju-se-yo)** - More, please

100. 도와주세요 **(do-wa-ju-se-yo)** - Please help me

101. 조용히 해 주세요 **(jo-yong-hi hae ju-se-yo)** - Please be quiet: *Quietly do please*

102. 기다려 주세요 (gi-da-ryeo ju-se-yo) - Please wait

103. 가자! (gaja) - Let's go!: *Go!*

104. [Something] 가요 (gayo)! - Let's go or Let's do [something]!: (When an idol yells out **"[Something] 가요 (gayo)!"** on stage, it generally means "Let's go!" in a polite and encouraging way. "가요" is used to hype up the audience and indicate that they are moving on to the next part of the performance.)

105. 와요 (wa-yo) - Come (here)

106. 같이 가요 (gachi gayo) - Let's go together: *Together go*

107. 집에 가요 (jibe gayo) - Let's go home: *Home-to go*

108. 잠시만요 (jam-si-man-yo) - Just a moment: *Moment only*

109. 잠깐만요 (jam-ggan-man-yo) - Just a second: *Second only*

110. 조심하세요 (jo-sim-ha-se-yo) - Be careful

111. 다시 말해 주세요 (da-si mal-hae ju-se-yo) - Please say it again: *Again say please*

112. 천천히 말해 주세요 (cheon-cheon-hi mal-hae ju-se-yo) - Please speak slowly: *Slowly speak please*

113. 가고 싶어요 (ga-go si-peo-yo) - I want to go

114. 하고 싶어요 (ha-go si-peo-yo) - I want to do

Now that we have covered the boring part, it is time to dive back into more K-pop fun! The next chapter is all about essential phrases that will enrich your fan experience.

Download your pdf and audio files for Chapter 8 - Everyday Phrases, using the QR code in the Intro.

NINE

K-POP PHRASES
THE FUN 130

SO YOU ARE WATCHING videos of your favorite idols on YouTube — footage from live concerts, interviews on TV shows, or fan service shows where you see and hear idols talking to fans or one another. After a while, you start to notice some phrases that are repeated frequently.

This chapter is going to cover those expressions that you are likely to hear over and over.

BEGNNINGS

Have you noticed certain filler words at the beginning of a conversation? They are the equivalents of "Well…" and "Okay, so…" Here are the two most commonly used ones in Korean:

"자, ..." (jah) is usually a way to grab attention and signal the start of something, similar to "Alright," "Well," or "Let's" in English.

For example:

- "**자,** 시작해볼까요?" (**Ja**, sijakhaebolkkayo?) - "Well then, shall we start?"
- "**자,** 다음 곡으로 넘어가요." (**Ja**, daeum gogeuro neomeogayo.) - "Alright, let's move on to the next song."

"그래, ..." **(geurae)** can be translated to "Okay," "Alright," or "Sure." It is used to confirm a statement, agree with someone, or express understanding.

For example:

- "그래, 알겠어." (**geurae**, algesseo.) - "Okay, I got it."
- "그래, 맞아." (**geurae**, maja.) - "That's right."

DIMINUTIVES OF ENDEARMENT

Have you ever noticed the idols call each other by names that sound slightly different from their actual names? That is because they are using "diminutives." This practice is commonly used among friends and family, and is similar to the way we call Jim "Jimmy" and Anne "Annie." Here are some ways Koreans do it:

1. Adding "-이" (i): This suffix is added to names ending in a consonant. For example, if someone's name is 태민 (Taemin), the nickname would be 태민이 (Taemin-i).

2. Adding "-아/야" (a/ya): For names ending in a consonant, use 아; for names ending in a vowel, use 야. For example, 태형 (Tae-hyung) → 태형아 (Tae-hyung-a), and 지수 (Ji-soo) → 지수야 (Ji-soo-ya). You would hear this when the speaker tries to catch the person's attention, as in "hey, [person's name]."

These diminutives are used to show affection and are especially popular among fans when they refer to their favorite K-pop idols.

THE 130 MOST COMMON PHRASES IN K-POP

Below are the 130 phrases most commonly used by idols and fans — in Hangul, romanized pronunciation, English translation, then *literal translation in italics* to help you understand how the sentence is constructed.

인사 (INSA) - GREETINGS AND FAREWELLS

1. **안녕하세요 (an-nyeong-ha-se-yo)** - Hello (polite): *Peace-do*

2. **안녕 (an-nyeong)** - Hi or bye (informal)

3. 여기 있어요 (**yeo-gi i-sseo-yo**) - I'm here/It's here: *Here (I) am/Here (it) is*

4. 다시 만나요 (**da-si man-na-yo**) - Let's meet again: *Again-meet*

5. 다음에 봐요 (**da-eu-me bwa-yo**) - See you next time: *Next time see*

6. 다음에 만나요 (**da-eu-me man-na-yo**) - See you next time: *Next time meet*

7. 다음에 또 만나요 (**da-eu-me tto man-na-yo**) - Let's meet again next time: *Next-time again meet*

8. 다음 공연에서 봐요 (**da-eum gong-yeon-e-seo bwa-yo**) - See (you) at the next performance: *Next performance-at see*

9. 잘자요 (**jal-ja-yo**) - Good night: *Well-sleep*

감사와 사랑 (GAMSA WA SARANG) - GRATITUDE & LOVE

10. 사랑합니다 (**sa-rang-ham-ni-da**) - I love you (formal)

11. 사랑해요 (**sa-rang-hae-yo**) - I love you (polite)

12. 사랑해 (**sa-rang-hae**) - I love you (informal): *Love-do*

13. 사랑해, 팬들 (**sa-rang-hae, paen-deul**) - I love you, fans: *Love-do, fans*

14. 사랑해요, 여러분 (**sa-rang-hae-yo, yeo-reo-bun**) - (I) love you, everyone: *Love-do, everyone*

15. 사랑받고 싶어요 (**sa-rang-bat-go si-peo-yo**) - I want to be loved: *Love-receive (I) want*

16. 감사합니다 (**gam-sa-ham-ni-da**) - Thank you (formal)

17. 고마워요 (**go-ma-wo-yo**) - Thank you (polite)

18. 고마워 (**go-ma-wo**) - Thank you (informal)

19. 정말 감사해요 (**jeong-mal gam-sa-hae-yo**) - Really, thank you: *Really-thank*

20. 여기 와주셔서 감사합니다 (**yeo-gi wa-ju-syeo-seo gam-sa-ham-ni-da**) - Thank you for coming: *Here come-give thanks*

21. 팬 여러분 덕분이에요 (**paen yeo-reo-bun deok-bun-i-ye-yo**) - It's thanks to you, fans: *Fan-everyone-thanks-to*

22. 함께해 줘서 고마워요 **(ham-kke-hae jwo-seo go-ma-wo-yo)** - Thank you for being with us

격려 (GYEONGNYEO) - ENCOURAGEMENT

23. 화이팅! **(hwa-it-ing)** - Fighting!/(We/you) can do it!!

24. 건강하세요 **(geon-gang-ha-se-yo)** - Stay healthy

25. 힘내세요 **(him-nae-se-yo)** - Stay strong: *Strength put-out*

26. 다들 힘내세요 **(da-deul him-nae-se-yo)** - Everyone, stay strong

27. 기다려 주세요 **(gi-da-ryeo ju-se-yo)** - Please wait for us

28. 믿어 주세요 **(mi-deo ju-se-yo)** - Please believe in us: *Belief please*

29. 기억해 주세요 **(gi-eok-hae ju-se-yo)** - Please remember us

30. 응원해 주세요 **(eung-won-hae ju-se-yo)** - Please support us

31. 앞으로도 잘 부탁드립니다 **(ap-eu-ro-do jal bu-tak-deu-rim-ni-da)** - Please continue to support us: *Future-also-well-ask*

32. 계속 지켜봐 주세요 **(gye-sok ji-kyeo-bwa ju-se-yo)** - Please continue to tune in/support us: *Continuously-watch-give*

33. 잘 부탁드립니다 **(jal bu-tak-deu-rim-ni-da)** - Please look kindly upon me going forward: This phrase is typically (though not exclusively) used when meeting someone for the first time in a professional setting, often directed to a client, partner, team that you will collaborate with, or even fans.

행복 (HAENGBOK) - HAPPINESS

34. 행복하세요 **(haeng-bok-ha-se-yo)** - Be happy: *Happiness-do*

35. 기쁩니다 **(gi-ppeum-ni-da)** - I'm happy (formal)

36. 기쁘네요 **(gi-ppeu-ne-yo)** - I'm happy (polite/infomal)

37. 오늘 정말 행복해요 **(o-neul jeong-mal haeng-bok-hae-yo)** - Today, I'm really happy: *Today-really-happy*

38. 여러분 덕분에 행복해요 **(yeo-reo-bun deok-bu-ne haeng-bok-hae-yo)** - I'm happy because of you guys/You make me happy

39. 감동이에요 **(gam-dong-i-ye-yo)** - I'm touched: *Touch-is*

40. 행복한 하루 되세요 (haeng-bok-han ha-ru doe-se-yo) - Have a happy day: *Happy-day-be*

공연 (GONGYEON) & 활동 (HWALDONG) - PERFORMANCE & ACTIVITIES

41. 즐기세요 (jeul-gi-se-yo) - Enjoy

42. 즐거운 시간 보내세요 (jeul-geo-un si-gan bo-nae-se-yo) - Have a good time

43. 준비됐어요 (jun-bi-dwaess-eo-yo) - Are you ready?: *Ready-became?*

44. 이 무대를 즐겨주세요 (i mu-dae-reul jeul-geo-ju-se-yo) - Please enjoy this stage: *This-stage-enjoy-give*

45. 다음 곡으로 넘어갈게요 (da-eum go-geu-ro neo-meo-gal-ge-yo) - We will move to the next song: *Next-song-to-move*

46. 열심히 연습했어요 (yeol-sim-hi yeon-seup-haess-eo-yo) - We practiced hard: *Diligently-practice-did*

47. 즐거웠어요 (jeul-geo-woss-eo-yo) - It was fun: *Enjoyable-was*

48. 오늘 즐거웠어요 (o-neul jeul-geo-wo-sseo-yo) - Today was really fun: *Today really fun-was*

49. 무대에서 봬요 (mu-dae-eseo bwae-yo) - See you on stage: *Stage-on-see*

50. 하지마 (haji-ma) - Don't do it/Stop it - *Do-not*

51. 농담이에요! (nong-da-mi-e-yo!) - Just kidding! I'm joking!: *Joke-it-is!*

계획 (GYEHOEK) & 약속 (YAKSOK) - PLANS & PROMISES

52. 계속 기대해 주세요 (gye-sok gi-dae-hae ju-se-yo) - Please keep looking forward to it: *Continuously-expect-give*

53. 열심히 하겠습니다 (yeol-sim-hi ha-get-seum-ni-da) - (I) will work hard/I will do (my) best: *Diligently-will-do*

54. 열심히 노력할게요 (yeol-sim-hi no-ryeok-hal-ge-yo) - I will try my best: *Diligently-effort-will-do*

55. 포기하지 않겠어요 (po-gi-ha-ji an-kess-eo-yo) - I won't give up: *Give-up-not-will*

56. 계속 열심히 하겠습니다 (gye-sok yeol-sim-hi ha-get-seum-ni-da) - I will continue to work hard: *Continuously-diligently-will-do*

57. 기대돼요 (gi-dae-dwae-yo) - I'm looking forward to it: *Expect-do*

단결 (DANGYEOL) - UNITY

58. 함께해요 (ham-kke-hae-yo) - Let's do it together/Let's be together/: *Together-do*

59. 우리 함께해요 (u-ri ham-kke-hae-yo) - Let's do it together/Let's be together

60. 우리 같이 해요 (u-ri ga-chi hae-yo) - Let's do it together: *We-together-do*

61. 우린 가족이에요 (u-rin ga-jo-gi-ye-yo) - We are family: *We-family-are*

칭찬 (CHINGCHAN) - COMPLIMENT/PRAISE

62. 잘했어요 (jal-haess-eo-yo) - Well done: *Well-did*

63. 최고예요 (choe-go-ye-yo) - This the best/You are the best

64. 팬 여러분 최고예요 (paen yeo-reo-bun choe-go-ye-yo) - Fans, you are the best/You guys are the best

65. 멋있어요 (meo-si-sseo-yo) - (You are/he or she is/they are) cool

66. 잘생겼어 (jal-saeng-gyeo-sseo) - (You are/he is/they are) handsome

67. 예뻐 (ye-ppeo) - (You are/she is/they are) pretty

68. 웃겨요 (utgyeoyo) - (You are/he or she is/they are) funny

69. 정말 섹시해 (jeong-mal sek-si-hae) - (You are/he or she is/they are) really sexy

70. 정말 재능이 있어요 (jeong-mal jaeneung-i isseoyo) - (You are/he or she is/they are) really talented

팬들이 하는 말 (PAENDEURI HANEUN MAL) - PHRASES FANS SAY

71. 나도 [이름] 사랑해요! (nado [ireum] saranghaeyo) - I love [name], too!

72. 최고야! **(choegoya)** - You're the best!

73. 대박! **(daebak)** - Woah! OMG!: *Big hit* (a slang for something shocking or amazing)

74. 컴백 언제야? **(keombaek eonjeya)** - When is the comeback?: *Comeback when-is?*

75. 응원해요! **(eungwonhaeyo)** - I support you!

76. 짱이야! **(jjangiya)** - This is the best!; you're the best

77. 콘서트/팬싸 가고 싶어! **(konseoteu/paenssa gago sipeo)** - I want to go to a concert/fansign!

78. 노래 좋아! **(norae joa)** - The song is great!

COMMON LINES/THEMES IN K-POP LYRICS

Love and Relationships

79. 사랑해 **(saranghae)** - "I love you"

80. 널 사랑해 **(neol saranghae)** - "I love you" (with an emphasis on "you")

81. 네가 좋아 **(nega joa)** - "I like you"

82. 좋아해 **(joahae)** - "I like you"

83. 함께 있고 싶어 **(hamkke itgo sipeo)** - "I want to be with you"

84. 널 원해 **(neol wonhae)** - "I want you"

85. 보고 싶어 **(bogo sipeo)** - "I miss you" (literally, "I want to see you")

86. 너 없이 못 살아 **(neo eopsi mot sara)** - "Without you, I cannot live"

87. 우리 사랑은 영원해 **(uri sarangeun yeongwonhae)** - "Our love is forever"

88. 첫사랑 **(cheotsarang)** - First Love

Heartbreak and Separation

89. 그리워 **(geuriwo)** - "I miss you"

90. 이별 **(ibyeol)** - Breakup/Parting

91. 기다렸어요 **(gi-da-ryeoss-eo-yo)** - "I have been waiting"

92. 널 잊을 수 없어 **(neol ijeul su eopseo)** - "I can't forget you"

93. 다시 돌아와 **(dasi dorawa)** - "Come back again" - *Again return*

94. 왜 떠났어 **(wae tteonasseo)** - "Why did you leave?" - *Why left*

95. 널 잊고 싶어 **(neol itgo sipeo)** - "I want to forget you"

96. 아파 **(apa)** - "It hurts"

97. 짝사랑 **(jjaksarang)** - Unrequited Love: *One-sided-love*

98. 실연 **(siryeon)** - Broken Heart: *Failed-relationship*

Dreams and Aspirations

99. 꿈을 꿔 **(kkumeul kkwo)** - "I dream"

100. 꿈을 꾸고 있어 **(kkumeul kkugo isseo)** - "I'm dreaming"

101. 니 꿈꿔 **(ni kkum-kkwo)** - "I dream about you"

102. 우린 할 수 있어 **(urin hal su isseo)** - "We can do it"

103. 날아오를 거야 **(naraoreul geoya)** - "I will soar"

104. 이뤄질 꿈 **(irwojil kkum)** - "A dream that will come true"

105. 포기하지 마 **(pogihaji ma)** - "Don't give up"

106. 희망을 가져 **(huimangeul gajyeo)** - "Have hope" - *Hope-particle have*

107. 목표를 향해 **(mokpyoreul hyanghae)** - "Towards the goal" - *Goal-particle towards*

108. 미래를 향해 **(miraereul hyanghae)** - "Towards the future" - *Future-particle towards*

Self-Empowerment and Confidence

109. 난 할 수 있어 **(nan hal su isseo)** - "I can do it"

110. 할 수 있어 **(hal su isseo)** - "I/We/You can do it"

111. 자신을 믿어 (**jasineul mideo**) - "Believe in yourself"

112. 강해져 (**ganghaejyeo**) - "Get strong"

113. 내 길을 가 (**nae gireul ga**) - "Go my own way"

114. 빛날 거야 (**bitnal geoya**) - "I will shine"

115. 포기하지 마 (**pogihaji ma**) - "Don't give up"

116. 널 믿어 (**neol mideo**) - "I believe in you" or "I believe you"

117. 날아올라 (**naraolla**) - "Fly high" - *fly-rise*

Unity and Togetherness

118. 너와 나 (**neowa na**) - "You and I"

119. 우린 하나야 (**urin hanaya**) - "We are one"

120. 함께 할 거야 (**hamkke hal geoya**) - "We will be together"

121. 네 곁에 있을게 (**ne gyeote isseulge**) - "I will be by your side"

122. 손을 잡아 (**soneul jaba**) - "Hold my hand"

123. 우리 함께라면 (**uri hamkkeramyeon**) - "If we are together"

124. 같이 가자 (**gachi gaja**) - "Let's go together"

Youth and Freedom

125. 청춘 (**cheongchun**) - "Youth" - (*Special note on* 청춘 - Consisting of 청, meaning "blue/green," and 춘, meaning "spring," this word has a special connotation that does not have an exact translation. It refers to the period of life from teenage years through young adulthood, characterized by unbridled passion and growth. It is portrayed as a time of exploration and self-discovery and celebrated for its fleeting beauty and infinite possibilities.)

126. 청춘이야 (**cheongchuniya**) - "It's youth"

127. 자유롭게 (**ja-yuropge**) - "Freely"

128. 끝까지 달려 (**kkeutkkaji dallyeo**) - "Run until the end"

129. 즐겨라 (**jeulgyeora**) - "Enjoy it"

130. 놀자 (**nolja**) - "Let's have fun"

. . .

Armed with these 130 phrases, you're now ready to decode the world of K-pop lyrics and interviews. Get ready to surprise yourself with how much you can understand!

Download your pdf and audio files for Chapter 9 - K-Pop Phrases, using the QR code in the Intro.

TEN
THE FINISHING TOUCHES
COMPARISONS, PREPOSITIONS, AND CONNECTORS

NOW THAT YOU know how to form simple affirmative sentences, questions, and negative sentences, you are well-prepared for your next trip to Korea. However, to achieve a more nuanced understanding of the language, we need to take your skills to the next level. Let's cover a few more areas.

COMPARISONS

As you attempt to communicate in Korean, pretty soon, you will feel the need to talk about relative qualities of people or things. You do not just want to say something is big, but you may want to say A is bigger than B, A is as big as B, or A is the biggest of them all. Let's take a look.

Comparative Sentences (More/Less)

To express that A is more/less than B, use the following rules.

Basic Structure:

A는/은/가/이 B보다 (boda) 더 (deo)/덜 (deol) **[Adjective]** — A is more/less [Adjective] than B.

- 더 **(deo)**: More
- 덜 **(deol)**: Less
- 보다 **(boda)**: Than

Example Sentences (polite form):

1. 더 (deo) - More

-(여자)아이들이 엔믹스**보다 더** 인기가 많아요. ((Yeoja) Aideuri Enmikseu-**boda deo** ingiga manayo.) - (G)I-DLE is more popular than NMIXX.

-이 책이 저 책**보다 더** 좋아요. (I chaegi jeo chaek-**boda deo** joayo.) — This book is better than that book.

-저는 여동생**보다** 신발이 **더** 많아요. (Jeo-**neun** yeodongsaeng-**boda** sinbari **deo** manayo.) — I have more shoes than my younger sister does.

- 저는 (jeo-neun) — I (with topic particle)
- 여동생보다 (yeodongsaeng-boda) — Than my younger sister
- 신발이 (sinbar-i) — Shoes (with subject particle)
- 더 (deo) — More
- 많아요 (man-ayo) — Have many / are many

2. 덜 (deol) - Less

-이 영화는 저 영화**보다 덜** 재미있어요. (I yeonghwa-**neun** jeo yeonghwa-**boda deol** jaemi-isseoyo.) - This movie is less interesting than that movie.

-친구가 저**보다** 덜 바빠요. (Chinju**ga** jeo-**boda deol** bappayo.) - My friend is less busy than I.

Comparative Sentences (Equal)

This form is used when you want to convey that A is as good as B.

Basic Structure:

A는/은/가/이 B만큼 (mankeum) + **[Adjective]** - A is as [Adjective] as B.

- 만큼 (**mankeum**): As...as

Example Sentences:

-이 책이 저 책**만큼** 좋아요. (I chaegi jeo chaek-**mankeum** joayo.) — This book is as good as that book.

-블랙핑크는 BTS만큼 유명해요 (Blackpink-**neun** BTS-**mankeum** yumyeonghaeyo) - BLACKPINK is as famous as BTS

Superlative Sentences

Superlatives express the highest degree of a quality. In Korean, you can form superlatives using 가장 **(gajang)** or 제일 **(jeil)**.

Basic Structure:

A는/은/가/이 가장 **(gajang)**/제일 **(jeil)** + **[Adjective]** - A is the most [Adjective].

- 가장 **(gajang)**: Most (literary)
- 제일 **(jeil)**: Most (conversational, colloquial)

Example Sentences

1. 가장 **(gajang)** - Most

-이 책**이 가장** 좋아요. (I chae**i gajang** joayo.) — This book is the best.

-씨엘은 **가장** 멋진 래퍼예요 (ssiel—**eun gajang** meotjin raepeoyeyo) - CL is the coolest rapper.

2. 제일 **(jeil)** - Most

-그 사람**이 제일** 빨라요. (Geu saram**i jeil** ppallayo.) — He/she is the fastest.

-이 노래는 앨범 중에서 **제일** 인기 있어요 (i norae-**neun** aelbeom jung-aeseo **jeil** ingi isseoyo) - This song is the most popular of the album.

Differences between 가장 and 제일

- 가장 **(gajang)**: It is often used in written language, formal speeches, and contexts where a more refined or official tone is preferred.
- 제일 **(jaeil)**: It is more commonly used in everyday conversation. It feels more casual and colloquial.

PREPOSITIONS

A preposition is a word that shows the relationship between a noun or pronoun and other elements in a sentence, indicating direction, location, time, or manner. We covered some of them — 에 (e), 에서 (eseo), 부터 (buteo), and 까지 (kkaji) — already under the section about particles in Chapter 4, but here are a few more important ones:

1. 위에 (wi-e): On, above

- 책상 **위에** (chaeksang **wi-e**) - On the desk.

2. 아래에/밑에 (arae-e/mit-e): Under, below

- 책상 **아래에** (chaeksang **arae-ae**) - Under the desk.

3. 옆에 (yeop-e): Next to, beside

- 학교 **옆에** (hakgyo **yeop-e**) - Next to the school.

4. 안에 (ane): Inside

- 가방 **안에** 책이 있어요. (Gabang **ane** chaegi isseoyo.) — There is a book inside the bag.

5. 밖에 (bakke): Outside

- 집 **밖에** 고양이가 있어요. (Jib **bakke** goyang-i-ga isseoyo.) — There is a cat outside the house.

6. 앞에 (ap-e): In front of

- 집 **앞에** (jib **ap-e**) - In front of the house.

7. 뒤에 (dwi-e): Behind

- 집 **뒤에** (jib **dwi-e**) - Behind the house.

CONNECTING SENTENCES

In any language, the ability to connect sentences and ideas is crucial for effective communication. As you progress, you will need more advanced grammatical structures to express complex ideas clearly and seamlessly.

Wouldn't it be cool if you could discuss your favorite idols' music, personalities, or performances in greater depth with fellow K-pop fans? Being able to connect sentences will allow you to engage in more meaningful discussions with fellow fans.

Let's explore various ways to link thoughts and express relationships between different sentences.

Conjunctions and Transitional Phrases

Conjunctions are words that join clauses and/or sentences together, while transitional phrases help indicate the relationship between ideas. These tools are indispensable for logical and fluent speech.

Here are some common conjunctions and transitional phrases in Korean:

1. 그래서 (geuraeseo) - So, therefore

- 그래서 저는 한국어를 열심히 공부해요 (**geuraeseo** jeoneun hangugeoreul yeolsimhi gongbuhaeyo) - So, I study Korean hard.

2. 그런데 (geurunde)/하지만 (hajiman) - But, however

- 저는 에스파를 제일 좋아하는데* 마마무도 좋아해요 (jeoneun eseupareul jeil joaha**neunde** mamamudo joahaeyo) - I like Aespa best, but I also like MAMAMOO.

* When placed between two phrases, the conjunctions are shortened to -는데 and -지만, and then attached to the (first) verb stem.

3. 그리고 (geurigo) - And, also

- 저는 노래 듣는 것을 좋아하고* 춤추는 것도 좋아해요 (jeo-neun norae deutneun geoseul joaha**go** chumchuneun geotdo joahaeyo) - I like listening to music, and I also like dancing.

*Same as the two conjunctions above, 그리고 is shortened to - 고 and then attached to the verb stem.

4. 때문에 (ttaemunae) - Because (of): This word comes *after* the cause/reason of the action, unlike in English.

- 저는 K-pop 때문에 한국 문화에 관심이 생겼어요 (jeo-neun K-pop **ttaemune** hanguk munhwae gwansimi saenggyeosseoyo) - I became interested in Korean culture because of K-pop.

Subordinate Clauses and Connectors

Subordinate clauses are dependent clauses that cannot stand alone as complete sentences but instead modify the main clause. They provide additional information or context. Connectors, on the other hand, are words or phrases used to introduce subordinate clauses and indicate their relationship to the main clause. Let's take a closer look.

Here are some common subordinate clauses and connectors in Korean:

1. -ㄴ/는다고 (-n/neun dago) - Indicates reported (indirect) speech

- 친구가 내일 콘서트에 **간다고** 했어요 (chinguga naeil konseote **gandago** haesseoyo) - My friend said that they are going to the concert tomorrow.

2. -면 (-myeon) - Indicates conditional clause

- 열심히 연습하**면** 너도 잘 출 수 있을 거야 (yeolsimhi yeonseupha-**myeon** neodo jal chul su isseul geoya) - If you practice hard, you will be able to dance well, too

3. -는 동안 (-neun dongan) - Indicates two or more concurrent actions (i.e. while, when)

- 청소 하**는 동안** 음악을 들어요 (cheongso ha**neun dongan** eumageul deureoyo) - While cleaning, I listen to music.

This concludes our lessons on basic mechanics and grammatical rules in the Korean language. While it takes time to master everything, you now have a solid foundation to build upon.

ELEVEN
THE REAL FUN BEGINS
PUTTING YOUR HARD-EARNED SKILLS TO WORK

AS A DEDICATED K-POP FAN, you have invested time and effort into learning the Korean language and culture. Now it is time to apply your skills and immerse yourself in the K-pop experience.

We have a feeling that the first thing you want to do — the thing you have been itching to do for the longest time — is sing along to your favorite songs, just the way they are supposed to sound, with confidence.

UNDERSTANDING K-POP LYRICS: UNRAVELING THE MEANING BEHIND THE MELODY

K-pop lyrics are more than just catchy tunes; they offer glimpses into the artists' lives, emotions, and the vibrant Korean society.

But let's face it—deciphering K-pop lyrics can be a bit daunting for non-native speakers. The rapid-fire pace, idiomatic expressions, and cultural nuances can make it feel almost impossible. Fear not! We are going to give you some strategies to help you crack the code, from dissecting song structures to identifying key vocabulary and themes. We will also share some helpful language learning and translation tools .

Breaking Down the Song Structure

The first step to mastering K-pop lyrics is getting to know the typical song structure. Most K-pop songs follow a familiar pattern, consisting of verse, chorus, and bridge. Recognizing these elements can help you anticipate recurring themes and vocabulary, making it easier to follow along.

1. **Verse:** This is where the story begins; each member showcases their vocal or rapping skills. The verses may feature more complex language and storytelling.
2. **Chorus:** The chorus is the heart of the song—catchy, repetitive, and emphatic. It drives home the message and is often the easiest part to sing along with.
3. **Bridge:** The bridge adds a twist. It introduces new ideas or emotions with a shift in the melody, tempo, or mood. This is where the song takes a fresh turn.

Understanding the overall structure helps us grasp the narrative more efficiently. Plus, repetition is your friend—recognizing repeated phrases can help you identify key themes.

Identifying Key Vocabulary and Themes

K-pop lyrics often revolve around universal themes and emotions. Familiarizing yourself with these themes is a great strategy if you are looking to connect more deeply with the songs you love.

1. **Recurring Words or Phrases:** Look out for words or phrases that keep popping up, like 사랑 (sarang) for "love," 꿈 (kkum) for "dream," or 희망 (huimang) for "hope." These often highlight the song's central theme.
2. **Emotional Expressions:** K-pop songs cover a spectrum of emotions, from joy to heartbreak and longing. Expressions like 행복해요 (haengbokhaeyo), meaning "I'm happy," 슬퍼요 (seulpeoyo), meaning "I'm sad," or 그리워요 (geuriwoyo), meaning "I miss you," can shape the song's mood.
3. **Cultural References:** Lyrics frequently include nods to Korean culture, history, and emergent social issues. Recognizing terms like 설날 (Seollal), Korean New Year, or 수능 (Suneung), aptitude tests similar to the SATs in the US, adds valuable context.

Sometimes, no matter how hard you try, a certain fragment of the lyrics might still elude you. Translation and language learning tools can be your secret weapons.

1. **Official Translations:** Many K-pop songs come with official translations provided by the artists or their agencies. (Just Google them.) While they might not capture every nuance, they give you a solid foundation.
2. **Fan Translations:** The K-pop community is full of dedicated fans who share their translations online. These can offer different interpretations and insights. Just remember to cross-reference for accuracy.
3. **Language Learning Apps:** Apps like Duolingo and Memrise have courses tailored for K-pop fans, integrating lyrics into their lessons. This makes learning vocabulary and grammar fun and relevant.
4. **Online Communities:** Engaging with K-pop fan communities and forums can provide invaluable insights. Sharing perspectives and expertise allows for a rich learning environment. Dive into discussions and don't hesitate to ask questions.

So, put on your favorite tracks, listen actively, and let the music guide you on an exciting adventure of linguistic and cultural discovery.

PRACTICING KOREAN WITH K-POP SING-ALONGS

Singing along to K-pop songs is a fun and effective way to practice Korean. Here are some tips to get you started:

Tips for Practicing

1. **Start with Familiar Songs:** Choose the songs you already love and know well. This makes it easier to focus on pronunciation and comprehension.
2. **Use Lyric Sheets or Video Subtitles:** Find the lyrics in Hangul and, if available, with romanization. Websites like Color Coded Lyrics provide detailed lyrics and translations. Follow the written lyrics as you sing along. Your eyes and ears will start to

connect the symbols with the sounds, and you will be able to understand what you are hearing more clearly.

3. **Repeat and Practice:** Sing the song multiple times. It can be overwhelming at first, but slowly but surely, you will improve. With repetition, you will get a good grasp of Korean pronunciation and learn to read faster.

4. **Break Down the Lyrics:** Say the lyrics out loud before singing along. This helps with accurate pronunciation.

5. **Understand the Meaning:** Learn the meanings of the lyrics by looking up new words and expressions. When you know what you're saying, you can pour your heart into singing with genuine emotion and connection.

Recommended Apps

1. **Smule:** This popular karaoke app lets you sing along to millions of songs, including K-pop hits. You can record your performances and even sing duets with other users. Smule comes with a scroll feature, which makes it easier to follow along.

2. **Kpop Pro:** This app offers a vast library of K-pop songs in Hangul with romanization and translation. It features AI listening technology for instant feedback on your pronunciation and includes video lessons from K-pop tutors and coaches.

3. **SOMESING:** A free karaoke app with hundreds of K-pop songs updated daily. It offers studio-quality sound and allows you to sing solo or duet with friends. SOMESING also provides tools to record and share your performances.

4. **StarMaker:** With StarMaker, you can sing karaoke songs with real-time pitch correction and vocal effects. The rolling lyrics help you with your sight-reading skills.

5. **YouTube Channels:** Channels like TJ Karaoke, Karaoke Stuffs, and Pandeaux offer a variety of K-pop karaoke videos with lyrics in Hangul and romanization. These channels frequently update their content, providing a wide range of songs to practice with.

Once you incorporate these tools into your practice routine, you will quickly see improvements in your Korean reading and pronunciation skills. So, grab your mic, pick your favorite K-pop song, and start singing your way to better Korean!

USING VIDEOS EFFECTIVELY

If you are like millions of K-pop fans worldwide, you probably spend countless hours on YouTube, immersing yourself in idol content: talk shows, music performances, behind-the-scenes clips, and official music videos. You've watched your favorite stars interact, share opinions, joke around, and just be themselves.

These videos are fun but can be challenging to follow. Your eyes dart between the subtitles and the idols' expressions and body language, trying to absorb every detail. It's a labor of love, but one that can be pretty exhausting.

Why not use these videos to improve your Korean skills? Try this method:

1. Find a video you like with Korean subtitles. (It can be a music video, but clips that show conversations and interactions are better.)
2. Watch once with English subtitles to understand the content.
3. Turn off the English subtitles and watch it again, listening while following the Korean subtitles. (Warning: It will be pretty brutal at first.)
4. Set the playback speed to 0.75, or even slower, so you can follow along while matching what you are seeing with what you are hearing.
5. When you are ready, start reading the subtitles out loud with the idols. Keep trying.

As you go through the process, you will discover your weaknesses and identify what you need to work on. Go work on it. Come back, and try again. Focus on one video at a time and keep it enjoyable - perfection isn't the goal. With regular practice, you'll soon catch more of those witty comments and inside jokes without translation!

ENGAGING WITH THE FAN COMMUNITY

The K-pop community is a vibrant, welcoming space—engage with fellow fans, share your passion, and make unforgettable memories!

Useful Phrases for Expressing Opinions and Emotions

When participating in fan discussions, whether online or in person, it is important to express yourself clearly and respectfully. Having a repertoire of useful phrases in Korean will help you convey your thoughts effectively.

Here are some key phrases:

1. I think...: 저는... 생각해요. (Jeoneun... saenggakhaeyo.)

  - Use this phrase to share your thoughts politely.

Ex: **저**는 이 노래가 정말 감동적이라고 **생각해요.** (**Jeoneun** i noraega jeongmal gamdongjeogirago **saenggakhaeyo.**) - I think this song is really touching.

2. In my opinion...: 제 생각에는... (Je saenggageneun...)

  - Use this phrase to express your take on a topic.

Ex: **제 생각에는** 이 안무가 제일 독특해요. (**Je saenggageneun** i anmuga jeil dokteukhaeyo.) - In my opinion, this choreography is the most unique.

3. I think so, too (I agree): 저도 그렇게 생각해요. (Jeodo geureoke saenggakhaeyo.) - *I-also that-way think.*

  - Use this phrase when you agree with someone.

Ex: 맞아요, **저도 그렇게 생각해요**. (Majayo, **jeodo geureoke saeng-gakaeyo**.) — Right, I think so, too.

4. I'm excited about...: ... 너무 기대돼요. (...neomu gidaedwaeyo.)

  - Express your excitement and enthusiasm for upcoming events or releases.

Ex: 이번 새 앨범 **너무 기대돼요!** (Ibeon sae aelbeom **neomu gidaed-waeyo!**) - I'm really excited about this new album!

5. I'm disappointed: 실망했어요. (Silmanghaesseoyo.)

  - Use this phrase to express your disappointment or dissatisfaction.

Ex: 이번 콘서트에서 제가 좋아하는 노래를 안 불러서 **실망했어요.** (Ibeon konseoteu-eseo jega joahaneun noraereul an bulleoseo **silmang-haesseoyo.**) - I was disappointed that they didn't sing my favorite song at this concert.

6. I'm happy/sad: 기뻐요/슬퍼요. (Gippeoyo/Seulpeoyo.)

- Use this phrase to express your emotions.

Ex: 우리 아이돌이 상을 받아서 정말 **기뻐요**! (Uri aidori sangeul badaseo jeongmal **gippeoyo**!) - I'm so happy that our idol won an award!

Navigating Online Fan Communities and Forums

Online fan communities and forums connect K-pop enthusiasts worldwide, allowing them to share content and discuss their favorite artists. These digital spaces form a vastly diverse global network.

Here are some basic guidelines for interacting with fellow fans:

1. **Respect others' opinions:** K-pop fandom is diverse, and fans may have varying opinions on artists, songs, and performances. Be open-minded and polite, even when disagreeing. Avoid personal attacks.
2. **Contribute meaningfully:** Share your unique interpretations of songs, music videos, or performances. Engage in constructive debates and provide evidence to support your arguments.
3. **Follow community rules:** Each online fan community has its own set of rules and guidelines to maintain a safe and welcoming environment for all members. Familiarize yourself with guidelines, respect moderators' decisions, and report inappropriate content.
4. **Collaborate:** Online fan communities provide opportunities to collaborate with one another on various projects, such as fan art, fan fiction, or song translations. Offer skills and provide constructive feedback.
5. **Stay informed:** Use communities to keep up with K-pop news and events. Follow reliable sources, verify information before sharing.

Dive into the exciting world of K-pop fandom, armed with your love for the music, your Korean language skills, and your desire to connect. Let your passion shine through in your interactions and create memories that will last a lifetime. The global K-pop community awaits you!

TWELVE
TOOLS & AIDS
BUILDING ON THE FOUNDATION

READING a book like this from cover to cover and understanding everything in it is one thing, but reaching the point where you can actually interact with native speakers is a whole different challenge.

So where will you go from here? How will you improve your vocabulary? How will you type messages to your favorites on Bubble or exchange ones with fellow fans? In this chapter, we are going to introduce some helpful tools.

But first things first, let's learn how to type Korean.

SETTING UP A KOREAN KEYBOARD

Before you can learn how to type Hangul, you need the right equipment/set up. Chances are, if you are not Korean, you probably don't own a computer with a Korean keyboard.

Assuming you are like most of us and are typing on a QWERTY keyboard, your first step is to add Korean as an "input language" on your computer.

For Windows:

1. Go to **Settings → Time & Language → Language**
2. Click **Add a Language**
3. Select **Korean**

4. Follow the prompts

Once you have your Korean keyboard set up, you can toggle between your regular English and Korean keyboards by:

1. pressing the **Windows** key and **Spacebar** together to switch back and forth, OR
2. clicking the input language option on the taskbar and select **Korean**

For Mac:

1. Go to **System Settings** → **Keyboard** → **Input Sources**
2. Click the + button to add a new input source
3. Select **Korean**
4. Select **2-set Korean** (3-set Korean is for Korean-dedicated keyboard, so it's probably not for you.)

To switch between different languages, either

1. Press **Command + Spacebar**, or
2. Click on the language option icon on the upper right corner and select **2-set Korean**

TYPING HANGUL

Once you have your Korean keyboard, you are all set to start typing Hangul. In Korean mode, this is how the keys are assigned to the Hangul characters:

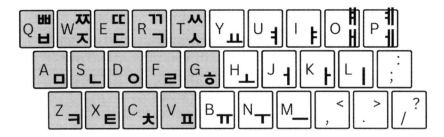

In Korean mode, type consonants and vowels as they appear on your keyboard. Notice that all the consonants are placed on the left hand

side and the vowels on the right hand side. Double consonants and diphthongs are accessed by the shift key.

Hangul syllables will automatically form as you type. For example, typing "ㄱ" then "ㅏ" will produce "가," and "ㅎ", "ㅓ," and "ㄴ" will produce "헌." Follow the basic left-to-right, top-to-bottom order as shown in the diagram below, and everything will fall into place. It is surprisingly simple.

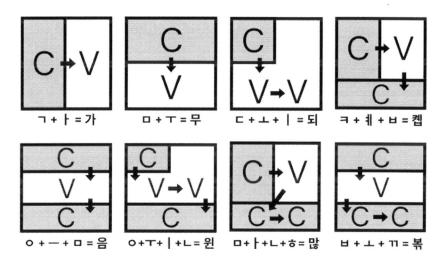

But how are you going to keep these key assignments straight? Well, you have three choices going forward:

1. Memorize the element-to-key assignment depicted above.
2. Get stickers that show both Koren and English alphabets to affix on each key.
3. Get a keyboard cover to place over your entire keyboard.

Option 1 is an admirable course of action, but Options 2 & 3 are much more practical — and available for under $10 on Amazon. Your choice.

If, for whatever reason, you cannot — or you don't want to — take the steps above and just want to type something in Korean NOW, go to Branah.com (https://www.branah.com/korean) and start typing away!

Practice Resources:

- **Online Typing Practice** - Websites like 10FastFingers offer Korean typing exercises to help improve speed and accuracy.
- **Typing Tutorials** - Websites like 90 Day Korean provide detailed guides and exercises for learning to type in Hangul.

ENABLING THE KOREAN KEYBOARD ON YOUR PHONE

To enable Korean keyboard on your phone, follow the simple steps below:

iPhone:

1. Go to **Settings** → **General** → **Keyboard** → **Keyboards** → **Add New Keyboard**
2. Search for **Korean** → **Standard**
3. Whenever you want to type in Korean, click on the globe icon in the bottom left corner until the Korean keyboard shows up.

Android:

1. Go to **Settings** → **General Management** → **Keyboard Settings** → **Languages and Types** → **Manage Input Languages**
2. Switch on **Korean**

LOOKING UP WORDS IN THE DICTIONARY

Using a Korean-English or English-Korean dictionary can help your learning. But let's face it, who's lugging around a bulky hard copy nowadays?

Luckily, we have all the resources we need at our fingertips. Some trusted online dictionaries and sources include:

- **Naver Dictionary** (https://korean.dict.naver.com/koendict/#/main): Naver offers one of the most comprehensive online Korean-English dictionaries.
- **Daum Korean-English Dictionary** (https://dic.daum.net/index.do?dic=eng): Daum offers similar features to Naver.
- **Papago** (https://papago.naver.com/): This excellent translation tool by Naver provides context and examples.

If all you have is your phone, here are your go-tos:

- **Naver Dictionary App:** Provides convenient access to the same features as the desktop version.
- **Papago App:** Great for on-the-go translations and learning.
- **Google Translate:** Useful for quick translations, though it may lack context and sometimes provide literal translations.

Tips for Effective Use of Online Dictionaries:

1. **Practice Pronunciation:** Use the pronunciation guides and audio examples.
2. **Learn Context:** Study example sentences to understand the correct context.
3. **Practice Regularly:** Frequently use the dictionary to build your vocabulary.
4. **Cross-Reference:** Use multiple dictionaries or translation tools to verify meanings, usage, and connotations.

OTHER ONLINE RESOURCES FOR LEARNING

The good news is, there is SO much out there; the bad news is, there is *too* much to choose from. Here is a list of tried and true resources to help you get started:

Websites:

1. Talk To Me In Korean (TTMIK)

talktomeinkorean.com: Offers comprehensive lessons from beginner to advanced levels, with audio, video, and written materials.

2. How To Study Korean

howtostudykorean.com: Provides structured and detailed lessons with thorough grammar explanations and vocabulary lists.

3. KoreanClass101

koreanclass101.com: Offers audio and video lessons with native speakers, covering various aspects of the language and culture.

4. Seoul National University Language Education Institute

lei.snu.ac.kr: Provides online courses and resources for Korean language learners.

5. FluentU

fluentu.com/:Uses real-world videos to create personalized language lessons with interactive captions and quizzes.

6. 90 Day Korean

90daykorean.com: Offers a structured course designed to teach you conversational Korean in 90 days with personalized coaching and comprehensive lessons.

YouTube Channels:

1. Talk To Me In Korean (TTMIK)

Talk To Me In Korean: Offers video lessons on grammar, vocabulary, and cultural insights.

2. Korean Unnie

Korean Unnie: Provides fun and engaging lessons on Korean language and culture, including K-pop related content.

3. Billy Go

Go! Billy Korean: Features lessons on Korean grammar, vocabulary, and speaking practice, with a focus on practical usage.

4. KoreanClass101

Learn Korean with KoreanClass101.com: Offers video lessons on various aspects of Korean, including pronunciation, grammar, and everyday phrases.

5. Sweet and Tasty TV

Sweet and Tasty TV: Provides entertaining videos on Korean language, culture, and food, often incorporating K-pop themes.

Apps:

1. Duolingo

duolingo.com: A popular language learning app that offers a fun, game-like format for learning Korean. It's great for beginners.

2. Memrise

memrise.com: Uses spaced repetition and mnemonic techniques to help users learn Korean vocabulary and phrases.

3. LingoDeer

lingodeer.com: Focuses on Asian languages, including Korean, and provides structured lessons with grammar explanations and practice exercises.

4. HelloTalk

hellotalk.com: A language exchange app where users can practice Korean with native speakers through text, voice, and video chats.

Books:

1. "Integrated Korean: Beginning 1" by Young-Mee Cho et al.

Part of the "Klear Textbooks in Korean Language" series, this book is widely used in university courses and provides a solid foundation in Korean.

2. "Korean Grammar in Use: Beginning to Early Intermediate" by Ahn Jean-myung and Lee Kyung-ah

A comprehensive guide to Korean grammar with clear explanations and practice exercises.

3. "Talk To Me In Korean Textbooks"

talktomeinkorean.com/books: These textbooks complement the TTMIK online lessons and are great for structured learning.

Online Communities:

1. Reddit - r/Korean

reddit.com/r/Korean: A community where learners and native speakers share resources, ask questions, and discuss all things related to the Korean language.

2. HelloTalk

hellotalk.com: Language exchange app where you can connect with native Korean speakers to practice conversational Korean.

K-DRAMAS:

In addition to the sing-along method discussed in the last chapter, we recommend you check out K-dramas — if you haven't already.

Turn off the English subtitles and turn on the Korean ones instead. Follow along the script with your eyes as you listen to the characters speak — basically doing the same thing as you would with K-pop songs and their lyrics but using just your eyes. Again, it will be overwhelming at first for sure, but as you keep doing it, you will gradually get better at it. We promise.

Watching K-dramas has become increasingly accessible thanks to various streaming services. Here are some popular platforms and methods for watching K-dramas:

Streaming Services:

1. Netflix

Netflix offers a wide selection of K-dramas, often with high-quality subtitles in multiple languages. Popular K-dramas on Netflix include "Crash Landing on You," "Itaewon Class," and "Kingdom."

2. Viki

Viki specializes in Asian dramas and movies, including a vast library of K-dramas. It provides community-contributed subtitles in many languages, making it a great option for international viewers.

3. Kocowa

Kocowa offers K-dramas, variety shows, and K-pop content. It's a joint venture by three major Korean broadcasters (KBS, MBC, and SBS) and provides high-quality subtitles.

4. Hulu

Hulu has a selection of K-dramas available for streaming. It's a good option if you already have a subscription and want to explore some Korean content.

5. Amazon Prime Video

Amazon Prime Video has a selection of K-dramas available, though its library is not as extensive as some other platforms.

Free Streaming Options:

1. YouTube

Some K-dramas are available for free on YouTube, either through official channels or with the permission of the broadcasters. Searching for the title of the drama might lead you to free episodes or clips.

2. Tubi

Tubi is a free streaming service that offers a selection of K-dramas with ads. It's a good option if you are looking for free content.

Cable and Satellite TV:

KBS World

world.kbs.co.kr/: KBS World is a Korean broadcasting channel available in many countries. It airs K-dramas with English subtitles, often shortly after they air in Korea.

Tips for Watching K-Dramas:

- **Check for Subtitles:** Ensure the platform offers subtitles in your preferred language.
- **Watch in HD:** For the best experience, choose platforms that provide high-definition streaming.
- **Explore Genres:** K-dramas come in various genres such as romance, thriller, fantasy, and historical. Explore different genres to find your favorites.
- **Join Online Communities:** Engage with other K-drama fans on forums, social media groups, and dedicated websites to discuss and get recommendations.

Hope we have given you enough to get started. Which way you go depends entirely on your personal preferences and comfort level with various platforms. It's all up to you, now, so go ahead, be creative, and have fun!

아웃트로/OUTRO
(YOU CAN READ THIS NOW!!)

LANGUAGE LEARNING IS A GRADUAL PROCESS, and it takes time and practice to master complex grammatical concepts and amass a decent-sized vocabulary. Embrace the challenge, celebrate your progress, and don't be afraid to make mistakes. With dedication and perseverance, you will soon be able to express yourself in Korean with greater fluency and confidence.

Remember that Korean people truly appreciate the effort when non-native speakers learn to communicate in Korean, however broken and imperfect it sounds. K-pop idols most certainly feel that way as they tour around the world and interact with their fans.

Don't be shy about making mistakes. They couldn't care less! Show your artists how much you love them. Wave hand-written Hangul signs and shout out fan chants in Korean. **They will most definitely love you back!**

부록 - APPENDIX

추가 어휘 - EXTRA VOCABULARY

음식-FOOD

밥 (BAP) - RICE

밥 (bap) - Cooked rice

비빔밥 (bibimbap) - Rice bowl with vegetables, meat, egg, and gochujang

돌솥비빔밥 (dolsot bibimbap) - Bibimbap in a hot stone pot

볶음밥 (bokkeum-bap) - Fried rice

김밥 (gimbap) - Korean-style rolls

불고기덮밥 (bulgogi deopbap) - Bulgogi rice bowl

오징어덮밥 (ojingeo deopbap) - Squid rice bowl

회덮밥 (hoe deopbap) - Raw fish rice bowl (similar to poke bowl)

알밥 (albap) - Fish roe rice

간장계란밥 (ganjang gyeran bap) - Rice with soy sauce and fried egg

잡곡밥 (japgokbap) - Mixed grain rice

누룽지 (nurungji) - Scorched rice (which has the texture of crunchy chips)

죽 (JUK) - PORRIDGES

전복죽 (jeonbok juk) - Abalone porridge

호박죽 (hobak juk) - Pumpkin porridge

팥죽 (pat juk) - Red bean porridge

닭죽 (dak juk) - Chicken porridge

면요리 (MYEON YORI) - NOODLES

라면 (ramyeon) - Korean instant noodles

냉면 (naeng-myeon) - Cold noodles

물냉면 (mul naengmyeon) - A type of 냉면, cold noodles in icy broth

짜장면 (jja-jang-myeon) - Korean-Chinese noodles with a sweet black bean paste sauce

잡채 (**japchae**) - Stir-fried glass noodles

칼국수 (**kalguksu**) - Knife-cut noodle soup

찌개 (JJIGAE) & 국 (GUK) - STEW & SOUP

찌개 (**jjigae**) - Korean stew

순두부찌개 (**sundubu jjigae**) - Soft tofu stew

탕 (**tang**) - Soup with clear broth

어묵탕 (**eomuk tang**) - Fish cake soup

감자탕 (**gamjatang**) - Spicy pork bone soup

알탕 (**altang**) - Spicy fish roe soup

매운탕 (**maeun tang**) - Spicy fish soup

연포탕 (**yeonpotang**) - Seafood, usually octopus, and vegetable soup

콩나물해장국 (**kongnamul haejangguk**) - Bean sprout soup

청국장 (**cheonggukjang**) - Fermented soybean paste stew

고기 요리 (GOGI YORI) - MEAT DISHES

불고기 (**bulgogi**) - Marinated and grilled meat

소불고기 (**sobulgogi**) - Marinated and grilled beef

갈비 (**galbi**) - Grilled beef short ribs

삼겹살 (**samgyeopsal**) - Grilled pork belly

제육볶음 (**jeyuk bokkeum**) - Spicy stir-fried pork

닭갈비 (**dakgalbi**) - Spicy stir-fried chicken

돼지고기 묵은지찜 (**dwaejigogi mugeunji jjim**) - Kimchi braised pork

수육 (**suyuk**) - Boiled pork belly

보쌈 (**bossam**) - Boiled pork belly with kimchi

떡갈비 (**tteokgalbi**) - Grilled short rib patties

산적 (**sanjeok**) - Skewered grilled meat

곱창 (**gopchang**) - Grilled intestines

돈까스 **(donkkaseu)** - "Tonkatsu," Pork cutlet

햄버거 스테이크 **(haembeogeo seuteikeu)** - Hamburger steak

해산물 요리 (HAESANMUL YORI) - SEAFOOD DISHES

해물 **(haemul)** - Seafood

해물찜 **(haemul jjim)** - Spicy steamed seafood

고등어구이 **(godeungeo gui)** - Grilled mackerel

생선구이 **(saengseon gui)** - Grilled fish

오징어볶음 **(ojingeo bokkeum)** - Spicy stir-fried squid

낙지볶음 **(nakji bokkeum)** - Spicy stir-fried octopus

오징어순대 **(ojingeo sundae)** - Squid stuffed with glass noodles

조개구이 **(jogae gui)** - Grilled shellfish

장어구이 **(jangeo gui)** - Grilled eel

아구찜 **(agu jjim) - Spicy braised monkfish**

해물파스타 **(haemul pasta)** - Pasta with seafood

간식 (GANSIK) - SNACKS

만두 **(mandu)** - Dumplings

군만두 **(gunmandu)** - Pan-fried dumplings

호빵 **(hoppang)** - Steamed buns

떡볶이 **(tteokbokki)** - Spicy stir-fried rice cakes

파전 **(pajeon)** - Savory pancake with green onions

반찬 (BANCHAN) - SIDE DISHES

김치 **(kimchi)** - Fermented vegetable dish

나물 **(namul)** - Seasoned vegetables

콩나물무침 **(kongnamul muchim)** - Seasoned soybean sprouts

감자조림 **(gamja jorim)** - Braised potatoes

계란말이 **(gyeran mari)** - Rolled omelet

계란찜 (**gyeranjjim**) - Steamed egg custard

계란후라이 (**gyeran hurai**) - Fried egg

장 (JANG) - FERMENTED SAUCE

된장 (**doenjang**) - Fermented soybean paste

고추장 (**gochujang**) - Fermented red pepper paste

간장 (**ganjang**) - Soy sauce

길거리 음식 (GILGEORI EUMSIK) - STREET FOOD

핫도그 (**hatdogeu**) - Korean-style hot dogs

토스트 (**toseuteu**) - Korean-style toast

샌드위치 (**saendeuwichi**) - Sandwiche

소떡소떡 (**sotteok sotteok**) - Skewered rice cakes and sausages

디저트 (DIJEOTEU) - DESSERT

호떡 (**hotteok**) - Grilled pancakes with honey filling

붕어빵 (**bungeoppang**) - Fish-shaped pastry with red bean filling

계란빵 (**gyeranppang**) - Sweet soft bread topped with egg

기본 동사 (GIBON DONGSA) - BASIC VERBS

하다 (**hada**) - to do

만들다 (**mandeulda**) - to make

가다 (**gada**) - to go

오다 (**oda**) - to come

있다 (**itda**) - to be; to have

없다 (**eopda**) - to be; to not have

되다 (**doeda**) - to become

살다 (**salda**) - to live

죽다 (**jukda**) - to die

동작 (DONGJAK)- MOVEMENTS

앉다 (**anda**) - to sit

서다 (**seoda**) - to stand

달리다 (**dallida**) - to run

걷다 (**geotda**) - to walk

타다 (**tada**) - to ride

수영하다 (**suyeonghada**) - to swim

날다 (**nalda**) - to fly

여행하다 (**yeohaenghada**) - to travel

출발하다 (**chulbalhada**) - to depart

도착하다 (**dochakhada**) - to arrive

나가다 (**nagada**) - to leave

들어가다 (**deureogada**) - to go inside

소통 (SOTONG) - COMMUNICATION

말하다 (**malhada**) - to speak

대화하다 (**daehwahada**) - to converse

설명하다 (**seolmyeonghada**) - to explain

가르치다 (**gareuchida**) - to teach

배우다 (**baeuda**) - to learn

공부하다 (**gongbuhada**) - to study

읽다 (**ilkda**) - to read

쓰다 (**sseuda**) - to write

물어보다 (**mureoboda**) - to ask

대답하다 (**daedaphada**) - to answer

인식 (INSIK) - PERCEPTION

보다 (**boda**) - to see / watch

듣다 (**deutda**) - to listen / hear

알다 (**alda**) - to know

모르다 (**moreuda**) - to not know

이해하다 (**ihaehada**) - to understand

기억하다 (**gieokhada**) - to remember

잊다 (**itda**) - to forget

찾다 (**chatda**) - to find / search

감정 (GAMJEONG) - EMOTION

사랑하다 (**saranghada**) - to love

싫어하다 (**sireohada**) - to dislike

좋아하다 (**joahada**) - to like

필요하다 (**piryo-hada**) - to need

필요없다 (**piryo-eopda**) - to not need

원하다 (**wonhada**) - to want

아프다 (**apeuda**) - to be sick/hurt

일상 (ILSANG) - ROUTINE (DAILY ACTIVITIES)

먹다 (**meokda**) - to eat

마시다 (**masida**) - to drink

자다 (**jada**) - to sleep

꿈꾸다 (**kkumkkuda**) - to dream

일어나다 (**ireonada**) - to wake up/get up

입다 (**ipda**) - to wear

벗다 (**beotda**) - to take off (clothes)

씻다 (**ssitda**) - to wash

목욕하다 (**mogyokhada**) - to bathe

샤워하다 (**syawohada**) - to shower

일 (IL) - WORK

일하다 (**ilhada**) - to work

운전하다 (**unjeonhada**) - to drive

청소하다 (**cheongsohada**) - to clean

요리하다 (**yorihada**) - to cook

운동하다 (**undonghada**) - to exercise

시작하다 (**sijakhada**) - to start

끝나다 (**kkeutnada**) - to finish

여가 (YEOGA) - LEISURE

만나다 (**mannada**) - to meet

기다리다 (**gidarida**) - to wait

놀다 (**nolda**) - to hang out/to have fun

쉬다 (**swida**) - to rest

전화하다 (**jeonhwahada**) - to call (phone)

방문하다 (**bangmunhada**) - to visit

초대하다 (**chodaehada**) - to invite

휴가를 보내다 (**hyugareul bonaeda**) - to vacation

그리다 (**geurida**) - to draw a picture

산책하다 (**sanchaekhada**) - to take a walk

기타 (GITA) - OTHER VERBS

주다 (**juda**) - to give

받다 (**batda**) - to receive

열다 (**yeolda**) - to open

닫다 (**datda**) - to close

만들다 (**mandeulda**) - to make

돕다 (**dopda**) - to help

사용하다 (**sayonghada**) - to use

짓다 (**jitda**) - to build

긋다 (**geutda**) - to draw a line

넣다 (**neotda**) - to put in

부르다 (**bureuda**) - to call, to sing

이기다 (**igida**) - to win

지다 (**jida**) - to lose

아이돌 관련 동사 (AI-DOL GWANRYEON DONGSA) - IDOL-RELATED VERBS

노래하다 (**noraehada**) - to sing

춤추다 (**chumchuda**) - to dance

랩하다 (**raep-hada**) - to rap

연주하다 (**yeonjuhada**) - to play an instrument

작곡하다 (**jakgokhada**) - To compose

가사 쓰다 (**gasa sseuda**) - To write lyrics

녹음하다 (**nogeumhada**) - To record

제작하다 (**jejakhada**) - to produce (records)

안무 짜다 (**anmu jjada**) - to choreograph

연습하다 (**yeonseuphada**) - To practice

춤연습하다 (**chumyeonseuphada**) - To practice dancing

리허설하다 (**riheoseolhada**) - to rehearse

준비하다 (**junbihada**) - to prepare, get ready

공연하다 (**gongyeonhada**) - To perform

촬영하다 (**chwaryeonghada**) - To film / shoot

데뷔하다 (**debwihada**) - To debut

홍보하다 (**hongbohada**) - To promote

사인하다 (**sainhada**) - to sign, autograph

팬사인회하다 (**paensainhoehada**) - To hold a fan signing event

인터뷰하다 (**inteobyuhada**) - To interview

연기하다 (**yeongihada**) - To act

음악방송하다 (**eumakbangsonghada**) - To perform on a music show

팬과 소통하다 (**paengwa sotonghada**) - To communicate with fans

농담하다 (**nongdamhada**) - to make a joke

놀리다 (**nollida**) - to tease

팬 관련 동사 [PAEN GWANRYEON DONGSA] - FAN-RELATED VERBS

따르다 (**ttareuda**) - to follow

응원하다 (**eungwonhada**) - to support, cheer

소리치다/소리지르다 (**sorichida/sorijireuda**) - to scream

외치다 (**oechida**) - to yell

형용사들 - ADJECTIVES

품질 (PUMJIL) - QUALITY

좋다 (jota) - to be good

나쁘다 (nappeuda) - to be bad

맞다 (matda) - to be right/correct

틀리다 (teullida) - to be wrong

다르다 (dareuda) - to be different

같다 (gatda) - to be the same

많다 (manta) - to be many, a lot

적다 (jeokda) - to be few, little

비싸다 (bissada) - to be expensive

싸다 (ssada) - to be cheap

재밌다 (jaemitda) - to be interesting, fun

재미없다 (jaemieopda) - to be boring

쉽다 (swipda) - to be easy

어렵다 (eoryeopda) - to be difficult

깨끗하다 (kkaekkeuthada) - to be clean

더럽다 (deoreopda) - to be dirty

능숙하다 (neungsukhada) - to be skillful

뛰어나다 (ttwieonada) - to be excellent

전문적이다 (jeonmunjeogida) - to be expert

재능있다 (jaeneungitda) - to be talented

놀랍다 (nollapda) - to be amazing

시끄럽다 (sikkeureopda) - to be loud

카리스마 있다 (kariseuma itda) - to be charismatic

예술적이다 (yesuljeogida) - to be artistic

창피하다 (changpihada) - to be embarrassing

신체 특성 (SINCHE TEUKSEONG) - PHYSICAL TRAITS

크다 **(keuda)** - to be big

작다 **(jakda)** - to be small

길다 **(gilda)** - to be long

짧다 **(jjalpda)** - to be short

키가 크다 **(kiga keuda)** - to be tall

키가 작다 **(kiga jakda)** - to be short (height-wise)

뚱뚱하다 **(ttungttunghada)** - to be fat

날씬하다 **(nalssinhada)** - to be slender (body-wise)

마르다 **(mareuda)** - to be skinny

무겁다 **(mugeopda)** - to be heavy

가볍다 **(gabyeopda)** - to be light

넓다 **(neolda)** - to be wide

좁다 **(jobda)** - to be narrow

깊다 **(gipda)** - to be deep

얕다 **(yatda)** - to be shallow

부드럽다 **(budeureopda)** - to be soft

딱딱하다 **(ttakttakada)** - to be hard

예쁘다 **(yeppeuda)** - to be pretty

아름답다 **(areumdapda)** - to be beautiful

귀엽다 **(gwiyeopda)** - to be cute

멋있다 **(meositta)** - to be cool, stylish

멋지다 **(meotjida)** - to be fashionable

잘생기다 **(jalsaenggida)** - to be handsome

날씨 (NALSSI) - WEATHER

덥다 **(deopda)** - to be hot

따뜻하다 **(ttatteuthada)** - to be warm

시원하다 (**siwonhada**) - to be cool

춥다 (**chupda**) - to be cold

습하다 (**seuphada**) - to be humid

건강 (GEONGANG) - HEALTH

건강하다 (**geonganghada**) - to be healthy

아프다 (**apeuda**) - to be sick, painful

피곤하다 (**pigonhada**) - to be tired

졸리다 (**jollida**) - to be sleepy

배고프다 (**baegopeuda**) - to be hungry

배부르다 (**baebureuda**) - to be full

감정 (GAMJEONG) - EMOTIONS

행복하다 (**haengbokhada**) - to be happy

슬프다 (**seulpeuda**) - to be sad

무섭다 (**museopda**) - to be scary / scared

화나다 (**hwanada**) - to be angry

기쁘다 (**gippeuda**) - to be glad

외롭다 (**oeropda**) - to be lonely

품성 (PUMSEONG) - PERSONAL ATTRIBUTES

예의 바르다 (**yeui bareuda**) - to be polite

겸손하다 (**gyeomsonhada**) - to be humble

정직하다 (**jeongjikhada**) - to be honest

똑똑하다 (**ttokttokhada**) - to be smart

게으르다 (**ge-eureuda**) - to be lazy

성실하다 (**seongsilhada**) - to be diligent

친절하다 (**chinjeolhada**) - to be kind

조용하다 (**joyonghada**) - to be quiet

시끄럽다 (**sikkeureopda**) - to be noisy

느긋하다 (**neugeuthada**) - to be relaxed

긴장하다 (**ginjanghada**) - to be nervous

멍청하다 (**meongcheonghada**) - to be stupid

용감하다 (**yonggamada**) - to be brave

겁쟁이이다 (**geopjaengiida**) - to be cowardly

화려하다 (**hwaryeohada**) - to be fancy / glamorous

단순하다 (**dansunhada**) - to be simple

기타 (GITA) - OTHER ADJECTIVES

중요하다 (**jungyohada**) - to be important

쓸모없다 (**sseulmoeopda**) - to be useless

유명하다 (**yumyeonghada**) - to be famous

특별하다 (**teukbyeolhada**) - to be special

평범하다 (**pyeongbeomhada**) - to be ordinary

성공하다 (**seonggonghada**) - to be successful

부사 - ADVERBS

갑자기 **(gapjagi)** - suddenly: Describes unexpected events.

Ex: 그 사람은 **갑자기** 떠났어요. (Geu sarameun **gapjagi** tteonasseoyo.) - "He/She left suddenly."

계속 **(gyesok)** - continuously, constantly: Indicates an action that continues without stopping.

Ex: 친구는 **계속** 통화 중이에요. (Chinguneun **gyesok** tonghwa jungieyo.) - "My friend is still on the phone."

조금 **(jogeum)** - a little, a bit: Used to indicate a small degree or amount.

Ex: 조금 더 주세요. (Jogeum deo juseyo.) - "Please give me a little more."

벌써 **(beolsseo)** - already: Indicates something that has happened earlier than expected.

Ex: **벌써** 끝났어요. (Beolsseo kkeutnasseoyo.) - "It's already finished."

이제 **(ije)** - now: Refers to the current time or moment, suggesting a transition into a new event.

Ex: **이제** 집에 가야 해요. (ije jibae gaya haeyo.) - "I need to go home now."

서로 **(seoro)** - each other, one another: Describes actions or feelings reciprocated between two or more people.

Ex: 우리는 **서로** 사랑해요. (urineun seoro saranghaeyo.) - "We love each other."

가끔 **(gakkeum)** - sometimes, occasionally: Indicates an action that happens from time to time.

Ex: **가끔** 외식을 해요. (gakkeum oesigeul haeyo.) - "Sometimes, I eat out."

아마 **(ama)** - probably, perhaps: Used to express uncertainty or likelihood.

Ex: **아마** 비가 올 거예요. (Ama biga ol geoyeyo.) - "It will probably rain."

절대로 **(jeoldaero)** - never (must be used with negative verbs): Used to emphasize a strong prohibition or negation.

Ex: 절대로 잊지 마세요. (Jeoldaero itji maseyo.) - "Never forget."

곧 **(got)** - soon: Indicates that something will happen in the near future.

Ex: 곧 올 거예요. (Got ol geoyeyo.) - "(They) will be here soon."

잘 **(jal)** - well: Describes doing something in a good or satisfactory manner.

Ex: 저는 잘 지내요. (Jeoneun jal jinaeyo.) - "I'm doing well."

역시 **(yeoksi)** - as expected, indeed, after all: Used to express that something has turned out as expected or to affirm a realization. It is often used in conversations by itself to mean, "I knew it!"

Ex1: 그 가수는 역시 최고예요. (Geu gasuneun yeoksi choegoyeyo.) - "That singer is, as expected, the best."

Ex2:

- **A:** 그 그룹이 상을 받았어요. (Geu geurubi sangeul badasseoyo.) - "That group won the award."
- **B:** 역시! (Yeoksi!) - "I knew it!"

참고 문헌 - REFERENCES

Talk To Me In Korean. (n.d.). Retrieved from https://www.talktomeinkorean.com

How To Study Korean. (n.d.). Retrieved from https://www.howtostudykorean.com

Seoul National University Language Education Institute. (n.d.). Retrieved from https://lei.snu.ac.kr

Innovative Language Learning. (n.d.). KoreanClass101. Retrieved from https://www.koreanclass101.com

FluentU. (n.d.). Retrieved from https://www.fluentu.com/korean

90 Day Korean. (n.d.). Retrieved from https://www.90daykorean.com

SPREAD THE K-POP LOVE!

안녕, K-Pop Fam! Congratulations, you made it to the end!

So, did this book help you level up your K-pop game? Do you feel closer to the heart of K-pop? Has your fan experience been enriched? Well, then…

Drop a quick review or even just a star rating and **help other fans find their way** to K-pop language awesomeness! It's super easy:

1. Just scan the QR codes below, which <u>will take you straight to the review page</u>, or go back to your order on Amazon and click on the "Write a product review" button.

2. Leave a star rating.

3. Share your thoughts on how this book helped you out. **Even a few words** can make a big difference!

Every review is like a fan chant - the more voices, the more epic it becomes! So, spread the K-pop love!

고마워요! (That's "thank you" - show off that new Korean swagger!)

The Hallyu Press Team

P.S. Bonus points if you sneak some Korean into your review. Make other fans go "대박!" (daebak!) 😊

If you would like to order another copy of this book, just scan: